AIM HIGHER WITH *PALGRAVE INSIGHTS IN PSYCHOLOGY*
Also available in this series :

978-0-230-24988-2

978-0-230-24986-8

978-0-230-27222-4

978-0-230-24944-8

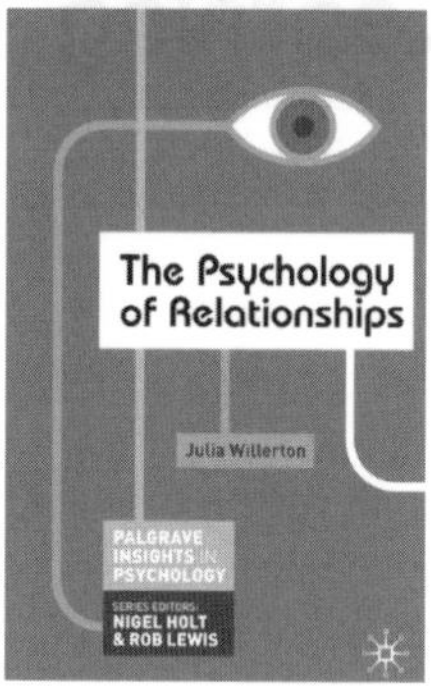

978-0-230-24941-7

978-0-230-25265-3

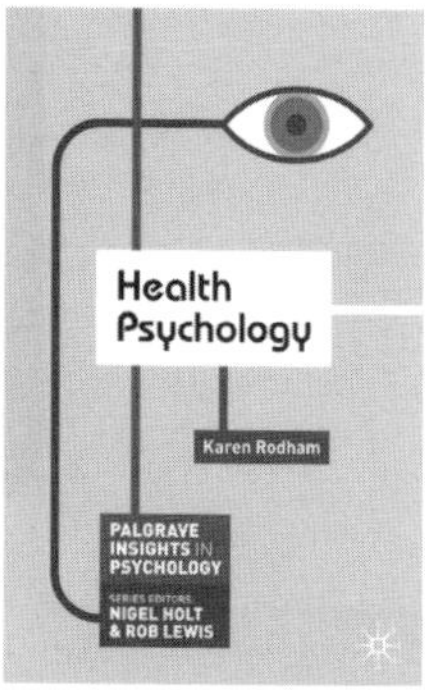

978-0-230-24945-5

978-0-230-24987-5

978-0-230-24942-4

To find out more visit
www.palgrave.com/insights

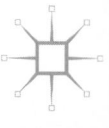

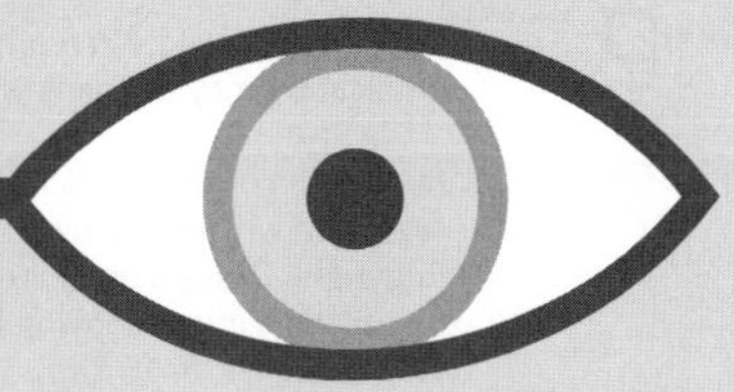

Intelligence and Learning

Nick Lund

PALGRAVE INSIGHTS IN PSYCHOLOGY

SERIES EDITORS:
NIGEL HOLT
& ROB LEWIS

palgrave macmillan

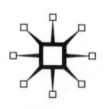

First published 2010 by
PALGRAVE MACMILLAN

Palgrave Macmillan in the UK is an imprint of Macmillan Publishers Limited, registered in England, company number 785998, of Houndmills, Basingstoke, Hampshire RG21 6XS.

Palgrave Macmillan in the US is a division of St Martin's Press LLC, 175 Fifth Avenue, New York, NY 10010.

Palgrave Macmillan is the global academic imprint of the above companies and has companies and representatives throughout the world.

Palgrave® and Macmillan® are registered trademarks in the United States, the United Kingdom, Europe and other countries.

ISBN: 978–0–230–24944–8

This book is printed on paper suitable for recycling and made from fully managed and sustained forest sources. Logging, pulping and manufacturing processes are expected to conform to the environmental regulations of the country of origin.

A catalogue record for this book is available from the British Library.

A catalog record for this book is available from the Library of Congress.

10 9 8 7 6 5 4 3 2 1
19 18 17 16 15 14 13 12 11 10

Printed and bound in Great Britain by
CPI Antony Rowe, Chippenham and Eastbourne

To Ellie and Daniel

Contents

List of figures and tables

Figures

Tables

Note from series editors

The study of intelligence is an important part of psychology and can sometimes be controversial. Discussions in both academia and the media over the years on topics such as the relationship between, for instance, race and intelligence, and the relative intelligence of males and females always encourage heated debate. Nick Lund takes us through the different areas of intelligence with great care and attention to detail, keeping a close eye on the sub topics and research that we expect to see.

Finding a writer prepared to tackle this topic should have been difficult. The breadth of the topic poses unique challenges to a writer developing a text within our strict guidelines. We were delighted to find that Nick Lund was keen to take on the task. He is an experienced writer and educator, and has worked at all levels, with knowledge of A-level right through to undergraduate degrees. His classroom and lecture theatre background are clear in his writing, and material presented in this book does not require translation or additional research but stands for all to read. It is Nick's enthusiasm and experienced delivery that drew us to him in the first place and he has produced another book to add to his not insignificant collection of work that will engage all those who choose to read it.

- *You may be reading this book as part of your preparation for university study.* Nick's experience as an undergraduate tutor and author, and his role as a consultant in teacher training mean that the material has been organized in way that is at the correct level, while remaining accessible and giving you, we hope, an appetite to take your study further.

- *Those reading the book while at university* will, no doubt, be reading additional books, perhaps others in this series, alongside this one. Nick's book develops and extends material on intelligence found in many introductory undergraduate textbooks and so can be regarded either in a supporting role or as a replacement for existing texts used in that area. Specialist books in intelligence are invariably extensive and can be somewhat dry, and Nick's interesting and engaging book is an invaluable companion to them.
- *If you are reading the book as part of a pre-university course such as A-level*, you will know from your A-level textbooks that intelligence is an important area in psychology. You'll find the material you need for your A-level in here and more besides. The Reading Guide at the end of the book tells you where different A-level specifications appear.

The majority of readers will, no doubt, be psychologists, but the study of intelligence finds a place in a wide range of disciplines including medicine, education and sociology. Whatever your area of study, or if you are reading simply for interest, we are confident that the book will inform and engage in equal measure and are proud to have it as part of the series.

Nigel Holt and Rob Lewis
Series Editors

Chapter 1

Introduction

This book is concerned with two concepts that are in common usage: learning and intelligence. We all have ideas about what learning is and what it means to be intelligent or, conversely, unintelligent. Psychologists tend to have specific meanings for the two terms but as we will see they do not all agree on the definitions. In fact, disagreements about the nature of intelligence lie at the heart of the debates discussed in later chapters. Learning, or at least the ability to learn, is often seen as evidence of intelligence. However, it is not the same as intelligence. Most animals are capable of learning and there have been a huge number of studies of it using animals from protozoa to humans (Pearce, 2008). However, many question whether non-human animals show intelligence. The study of human intelligence and the development of tests of intelligence have not only generated a vast amount of work but also caused the greatest controversy. Intelligence tests can be seen as the most successful tool developed by psychology or its greatest folly. This chapter introduces these two concepts before going on to explore them in detail in subsequent chapters.

This chapter will cover:

- What is learning?
- What is intelligence?
- Problems of studying animal learning and intelligence
- Problems of studying human intelligence

What is learning?

Learning is important. Most human behaviour results from some form of learning. Eichenbaum (2008, p. 2) claims that 'our individual personalities and intellect result from a lifetime of learning'. This view suggests we are what we learn. Furthermore, learning is always in progress and is always helping us adapt to our environment (Bouton, 2007).

We all have an idea of what learning is but, as Pearce (2008) points out, it is very hard to define clearly. He suggests (p. 13) that learning occurs 'when some experience results in a relatively permanent change in the reaction to a situation'. This definition contains a number of important elements. The first is that learning is the result of experience (that is, behaviour changes because of something happening to us). There are many factors that might change behaviour which would not be classed as learning. For example, behaviour might change because of fatigue. Tired people behave differently but this is not learned. Behaviour may also change because of disease. However, if you start sneezing tomorrow you have not suddenly learned sneezing behaviour. There are also some changes to behaviour that are due to maturation: for example when young males talk and sing in a high-pitched voice but during adolescence their voices change to a lower pitch. This is not learned but is the result of getting older. A change in behaviour is only regarded as learning if it is due to experience or to environmental stimuli. The other element of the definition is that learning should be a relatively permanent change in the reaction to a situation. In other words learning is not a momentary reaction to a stimulus but is a stored response that occurs repeatedly over time.

Eysenck (2004) notes that when psychology emerged as a scientific discipline the major focus of research was the study of learning. This early research focused on relatively simple forms of learning such as conditioning. This type of learning is the focus of Chapter 2. Later studies of learning tended to concentrate on more complex forms of learning involving information processing and intelligence. These are considered in subsequent chapters.

What is intelligence?

The question 'what is intelligence' is a central issue throughout this book. This question lies at the heart of most of the debates about intelligence and intelligence testing. The problem is there is no one universally agreed definition of intelligence. As Bartholomew (2004, p. 1) notes 'Almost everyone uses the word intelligence but it is one of those

Humpty Dumpty words whose meaning is so elastic that it can cover virtually anything we choose'. Intelligence is a complex concept that encompasses a lot of human and animal behaviour. One source of confusion is deciding which behaviours or abilities should be considered intelligent. Should intelligence be regarded as the ability to use verbal information or should it be the ability to solve problems? Alternatively should someone who is skilful in dealing with others be regarded as intelligent?

Gardner (2002) suggests a second source of confusion about intelligence is that the term has at least three meanings. The first is 'intelligence as species characteristic'. This meaning is about intelligence as a species-specific ability and looks at differences between species and evolution of intelligence. This is dealt with in Chapters 3, 4 and 5. The second meaning is 'intelligence as individual difference'. This is more concerned with quantifying intelligence to establish different levels of intelligence among individuals. This meaning is the subject of Chapter 7. The third meaning is 'intelligence as fit execution of a task or role'. This refers to the ability to carry out tasks well in a given environment.

Gardner suggests the individual difference approach tends to be about 'computing power'. He points out that people may be equal in terms of computing capacity but very different in their performance of a task (for example, two doctors might have the same IQ but one may give consistently more accurate diagnoses). Gardner claims this meaning is least used by psychologists but is one that deserves more attention. To avoid confusing the first of Gardner's two meanings, it is worth examining animal and human intelligence separately.

What is animal intelligence?

Animal intelligence cannot be defined in the same way as human intelligence. This is partly because a range of abilities regarded as signs of intelligence in humans, such as linguistic and numerical skills, are not found in animals. Pearce (2008) discusses three characteristics that could be used to define animal intelligence: adaptability, learning and information processing. He suggests that, for a number of researchers, adaptability is the defining characteristic of intelligence. However, the concept of adaptability is difficult to measure. Is an ant less adaptable than a chimpanzee if they are both surviving in the same forest? The notion of adaptability also does not identify the mechanism that allows an animal to adapt. One solution to this is to study the ability of animals to learn about their environment. During the early twentieth century it was assumed that animals that learn faster or learned more were more intelligent (Warren, 1973). However, this appears to be misguided. There is a lot of evidence that neither speed nor quantity of learning is linked to intelligence. Pearce (2008) points out that evidence shows that humans learn complex mazes at about the same speed as a rat and in some circumstances fish learn faster than rats. Furthermore, the amount any species is able to learn depends upon what is being learned and the context. Pearce suggests a better measure of intelligence might be the ability to use learning to solve problems. This involves using processing of information.

The topic of animal intelligence tends to be concerned with different questions to that of human intelligence. Instead of the preoccupation of what intelligence is and how it can be measured, comparative psychologists tend to question whether animals show evidence of intelligence and if so, which species show more or less intelligence.

What is human intelligence?

The simple answer to this question is it depends who you ask! A number of studies have examined non-expert or laypersons' views on the nature of intelligence. For example, Sternberg, Conway, Ketron and Bernstein(1981) studied the views of people in the USA. They asked over 180 people from three locations to list behaviours that were intelligent and unintelligent. Later, 120 other people rated how these behaviours related to intelligence. The findings suggest people in the USA regard intelligence as having three dimensions: practical problem solving, verbal ability and social competence. Studies of other cultures reveal a different conception of intelligence. Yang and Sternberg (1997) sought the views of Taiwanese Chinese people and found that in this sample five dimensions of intelligence emerged. These included some that were similar to those in the USA, such as problem solving and interpersonal intelligence but also some that were different. These include intrapersonal intelligence (using knowledge about oneself), intellectual self-assertion (confidence in one's knowledge and ability) and intellectual self-effacement (modesty and humility). Sternberg and Kaufman (1998) believe there are differences in views on intelligence between individualistic cultures (for example the USA and Western Europe) and collectivist cultures (for example Asia and Africa). Notions of intelligence in individualistic cultures tend to be focused on what individuals are capable of whereas in collectivist cultures the focus is more social.

The definitions of human intelligence given by experts also vary. For example, Sternberg and Detterman (1986) asked for the views of 24 experts and found many different definitions including problem solving, abstract thinking and originality. Similarly, Jensen (1998) found that a number of experts all gave a different definition of intelligence. The nature of intelligence and the problem of defining it will be considered in detail in Chapter 6.

Problems of studying animal learning and intelligence

There are a number of problems encountered when studying animal learning and intelligence. As with human studies, learning and intelligence in animals cannot be directly observed. However, in animal studies there is an additional problem of communication. Much of our understanding of intelligence in humans and the tests to assess it are based on the use of language. Animals do not have language; consequently the existence of learning or intelligence has to be inferred from their behaviour. Therefore, one major problem of any evidence is that it is based on interpretation. There are three other problems in this area **anthropomorphism**, animal senses and animal diversity.

Interpretation of evidence

One of the main problems in studying animal learning and intelligence is that they are not directly observable. We cannot see learning or intelligence but have to infer them from observations of an animal's behaviour. However, using animal behaviour as evidence of such mental processes can be difficult. Behaviours can often be explained in very different ways. For example, some apes have been taught to use sign language (see Chapter 4). One way of interpreting the signs that they use is that they have learned to use and understand a form of language. However, there is an alternative explanation. This is that they have learned a series of actions to get rewards such as food (see Operant conditioning in Chapter 2) and that this does not require any concept of language.

Thinking scientifically → **Clever Hans, the horse who could count**

One of the earliest studies of animal intelligence was carried out in the early 1900s on 'Clever Hans', a horse (Pfungst, 1965). Hans's owner claimed that the horse could count and was able to perform mathematical calculations. When given a problem to solve, the horse gave the answer by striking its hoof on the ground. So if asked what is two plus two, Hans would strike the ground four times. Hans seemed to be able to solve a variety of problems including additions, subtractions, multiplications and divisions.

There was understandable scepticism about these claims and a committee was established to investigate them. To their surprise, the committee initially found that the claim was true. When Hans's trainer set a mathematical problem, the horse usually gave the correct response. Hans seemed to be a numerate horse that could understand problems posed in a human language. However, further investigation revealed a different explanation of the horse's behaviour. Close observation of both the horse and the trainer showed that when Hans reached the correct number of hoof strikes for a particular problem the trainer's expression changed slightly. This slight change, lifting the eyebrows, was a cue to Hans to stop. When he did so, he was rewarded with food. When the trainer's face was hidden, Hans gave random responses.

Hans was able to respond to very subtle cues to obtain food but could not count.

Anthropomorphism

When analysing the behaviour of animals it is tempting to explain the behaviour in human terms. If you have a cat that rubs against your legs when its food bowl is empty it is tempting to conclude that the cat is 'feeling' hungry and 'thinking' about food. When studying some of the complex behaviour shown by animals in both laboratory studies and their natural habitat, it is difficult not to explain it in terms of thinking. However, emotions, thoughts and consciousness are human attributes that we can share with other humans using language. We cannot know whether animals share a similar experience. Explaining animal behaviour using human characteristics is called anthropomorphism.

The example of Clever Hans shows how anthropomorphism can lead to a complete misinterpretation of an animal's behaviour. In that case the trainer used a human ability, to do mathematics, to explain the horse's behaviour. Examples like these led one of the early comparative psychologists, Lloyd Morgan (1894) to suggest that no animal behaviour should be explained in terms of complex mechanisms (for example thinking) if it could be explained by simpler processes (for example **conditioned responses** and so on). This is known as **Lloyd Morgan's Canon**. In the case of Clever Hans the horse's behaviour was initially explained by a complex mental process (counting) but it was shown that it was explained better by a simpler process (a conditioned response to visual cues).

As we will see in later chapters, psychologists try hard to avoid anthropomorphism. They strive to be objective by devising experiments that provide unambiguous evidence of animals' abilities. However, some researchers believe this has led to a different difficulty. For example, Fisher (1996) argues that the dangers of anthropomorphism are overstated and that the requirement to explain behaviour in the simplest form leads us to disregard and underestimate the capabilities of animals. Fisher claims the ' charge of anthropomorphism oversimplifies a complex issue – animal consciousness – and it tries to inhibit consideration of positions that ought to be evaluated in a more open-minded and empirical manner'. Thus, in striving to avoid anthropomorphism, researchers may be ignoring evidence that animals do have similar cognitive abilities as humans.

Animal senses

Another problem of relying on the interpretation of animals' responses to infer learning and intelligence is that they may not respond to the same stimuli as humans. There are four possible sources of confusion. Firstly, some animals may sense information that is beyond the range of human detection. Pigeons, for example, can detect sounds at frequencies well below the range of humans (Yodlowski, Kreithen and Keeton, 1977). Similarly some animals detect different light frequencies to humans and some detect a different range of odours and tastes. The second problem is that an animal may sense information that humans are not able to detect at all. For example, some fish use electric fields to detect other animals (Lissman, 1963). The third problem is that animals may not detect stimuli that humans can sense. Finally, animals may produce responses to stimuli that go unnoticed by humans. Dolphins, for example, can produce high frequency sounds that humans cannot detect unaided.

Animal diversity

A further problem of discussing 'non-human animals' is that this phrase refers to millions of species. Any discussion of learning or intelligence in non-human animals cannot encompass the diversity found in the animal kingdom. There is such variation in factors such as nervous systems, social complexity and environment that it is not possible to make sweeping statements about non-human animals. The intelligence of a mammal such as the chimpanzee is difficult to compare to that of an insect such as the honeybee. One of the main questions is whether non-human animals show evidence of intelligence, therefore the evidence in Chapters 3 and 4 concentrates on those species most likely to show it: apes and cetaceans (aquatic mammals).

Dealing with problems posed by animal studies

Most of the problems outlined above stem from difficulties caused by interpretation of animal behaviour. The evidence can be open to conflicting explanations of the behaviour. Pearce (2008) suggests there are two ways of choosing between conflicting explanations, the first is based on theory and the second is based on the use of the experimental method.

The theoretical answer is to use Lloyd Morgan's Canon. If the evidence points to two conflicting explanations then the explanation using the simpler processes should be accepted. For example, if a behaviour can be explained by both a relatively simple process such as conditioning and a more complex process such as imitation, then the conditioning explanation should be accepted. However, there are dangers inherent in this approach. The assumption that the explanation using the simpler process is correct may cause comparative psychologists to ignore evidence of higher psychological processes.

The second approach is to use the experimental method. Popper (1959) suggests that science progresses in a research cycle where the problems found by one study are used to generate new hypotheses which are tested by further experiments. Thus if the evidence from one study of animal learning or intelligence is ambiguous then this should be investigated with further experiments. Although this seems like a simple solution, it is difficult to devise studies that demonstrate a mental process unambiguously. Shettleworth (1998) points out that 'formulating unambiguous alternatives does not guarantee finding unambiguous answers'. This is complicated by the uncertain nature of the concepts being studied. It is hard to demonstrate unambiguous evidence for something like intelligence or language that does not have unambiguous definitions.

Problems of studying human intelligence

Like animal intelligence, human intelligence is not directly observable. It is a hypothetical construct that we infer from behaviour and tests. However, unlike the study of animal intelligence, the major problems of studying human intelligence are not practical but ethical and moral problems. The study of human intelligence and, in particular, comparisons of human intelligence has proved to be the most divisive issue in psychology. Psychologists have devised psychometric tests to try to measure and quantify intelligence. This has led to claims that intelligence is different between various groups and populations. The controversy this caused has spread beyond the pages of academic journals to front pages of newspapers. The claims and counterclaims of those believing that intelligence differences are genetic, environmental or cultural artefacts are one of the most heated debates in modern science.

Part of the problem is that the psychologists are dealing with a socially sensitive issue. The question of intelligence differences deals with cultural issues, ethnic groups, social class and gender issues. The science of psychology became embroiled in a political debate and ideology. The findings of the psychologists had implications for resourcing education, social policy and other issues. The issues involved are illustrated in the controversy that followed the publication of a book called *The Bell Curve: Intelligence and Class Structure in American Life* by Herrnstein and Murray (1994). They suggested that there were differences between various groups that were caused by genetic factors. The issues surrounding these claims are discussed in Chapter 7.

Note

It is cumbersome to always refer to 'non-human' animals so in subsequent chapters the terms animal and human will be used unless there is potential for confusion.

Further reading

Gardner, H., Kornhaber, M.L. and Wake, W.K. (1996) *Intelligence: Multiple Perspectives*. Fort Worth, TX: Harcourt Brace College.

Maltby, J., Day, L. and Macaskill, A. (2007) *Personality, Individual Differences and Intelligence*. Harlow: Pearson Prentice Hall.

Pearce, J.M. (2008) *Animal Learning and Cognition: An Introduction* (3rd edn). Hove: Psychology Press.

Chapter 2

Animal learning

Animals, including humans, are faced with a huge range of stimuli each day. In order to survive, animals must respond to some of these stimuli. Some stimuli will be signs of predators, some might be linked to food or water, while other stimuli might indicate the direction of shelter. These different stimuli become linked to different behaviours. In other words, animals learn to respond to them. This applies to humans as well. For instance, as I drive home tonight I will stop my car if I see a red traffic light in my path but if the light is green, I will carry on. This form of learning, when a stimulus is linked to a subsequent behaviour, is known as associative learning. Associative learning theories were developed by behaviourists and are often described as stimulus–response theories (S–R). Skinner (1938) made a distinction between two different types of associative learning. One type results in a behaviour that is automatically elicited by a stimulus (which he called 'respondent' behaviour) and another in a voluntary behaviour that is governed by its consequences (which he called 'operant' behaviour). There are two behaviourist explanations of learning: classical conditioning, which deals with respondent behaviour, and operant conditioning, which deals with operant behaviour.

This chapter will cover:

- Classical conditioning
- Evaluation of the role of classical conditioning in the behaviour of animals
- Operant conditioning
- Evaluation of the role of operant conditioning in the behaviour of animals
- Problems of associative learning theories

Classical conditioning

Classical conditioning was first described by Pavlov (1927) in one of the most famous serendipitous findings in psychology. Pavlov was not a psychologist but a physiologist who was interested in reflexes such as salivation. Salivation is an innate **reflex** that occurs when food is placed in the mouth. Animals have a range of these reflexes and they are characterized by being involuntary and automatic responses to stimuli, which are not altered by experience (that is, they are not learned). However, in a study of salivation in dogs Pavlov found that this reflex was altered by experience; he found evidence of learning. Pavlov had developed an accurate way of recording the amount of saliva the dogs produced and found that they often salivated before the food was in their mouths (that is, it was not the normal reflex). They seemed to be responding to stimuli that were linked to the food such as the sight of food bowls, the sound of food being prepared and so on. These stimuli did not originally trigger salivation but after a while they did. The dog's behaviour had changed as a result of their experience; they had learned to respond to other stimuli.

These findings led Pavlov to begin a series of studies to investigate how this learning had occurred. He found that responses that had previously been triggered by one stimulus could be triggered by another after a period of learning (or conditioning) in a process now known as classical conditioning. In his most well-known study Pavlov conditioned dogs to salivate to the sound of a bell. At the beginning of the study he tested the effect of two different stimuli: food in the mouth and the sound of a bell. The food triggered salivation as it is a reflex which does not require conditioning. Since this was unlearned, or unconditioned, the food was labelled as an **unconditioned stimulus** (UCS) and the salivation as an **unconditioned response** (UCR). During this stage the sound of the bell did not trigger the salivation reflex and was labelled a neutral stimulus. The next stage of the study involved pairing the food with the sound of the bell a number of times. Since this eventually led to a change of behaviour this process is called conditioning. The final stage was to ring the bell in the absence of food. Pavlov found that this previously neutral stimulus now triggered the response of salivation. The dog had learned to salivate to the sound of a bell. As this was learned, or conditioned, the bell was now a **conditioned stimulus** (CS) and the salivation a

conditioned response (CR). The general process of classical conditioning is shown in Figure 2.1.

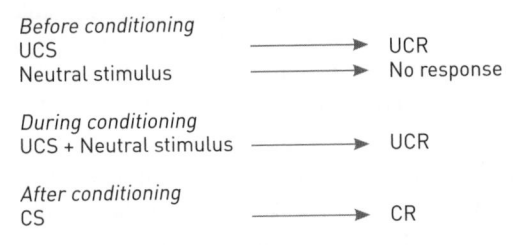

Before conditioning	
UCS →	UCR
Neutral stimulus →	No response
During conditioning	
UCS + Neutral stimulus →	UCR
After conditioning	
CS →	CR

Figure 2.1 General process of classical conditioning

This general process applies to all classical conditioning procedures and many reflexes can be linked to new stimuli in this way. One reflex that has been studied extensively in animals and humans is blinking (Eichenbaum, 2008). A puff of air onto the eyeball (UCS) causes the eye to blink (UCR). If the puff of air is paired with another stimulus such as a tone then eventually the tone will trigger blinking. The tone has become the CS and the blinking is now a CR. Although this example may not seem very relevant to animal learning in the natural environment, classical conditioning can be used to explain behaviours as diverse as diet choice in animals to phobias in humans.

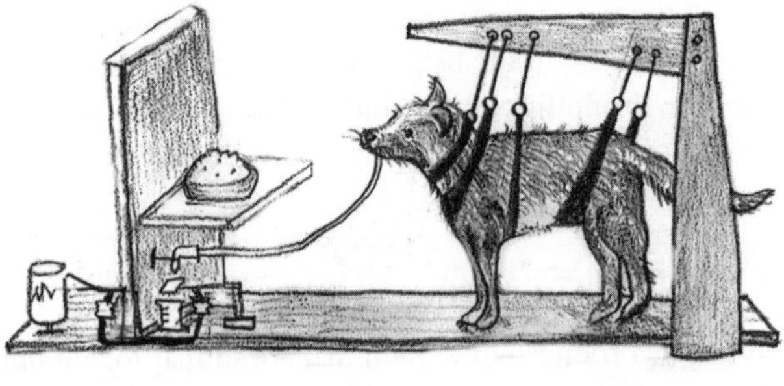

Figure 2.2 Pavlov's original apparatus The dog is restrained in a sling. The volume of saliva produced is recorded on paper on a rotating drum. (Illustration: Bryony Budd)

Extinction and spontaneous recovery

The UCRs associated with reflexes do not change or fade with the repeated presentation of a UCS. A puff of air onto the eye will cause the blink reflex over a period of months or years. In contrast Pavlov found that conditioned responses do fade if the CS is presented alone (that is, without pairing it to the UCS). When the CS is presented by itself repeatedly the CR becomes weaker and weaker until it stops completely. Pavlov called this process **extinction**. In his study, when the bell (the CS) was rung repeatedly without any food the dogs stopped salivating (the CR) to the sound of the bell.

The term extinction implies that the CR disappears completely but usually this is not the case and it often comes back without further conditioning. If the CS is not presented for a while after extinction and then presented again, the CR can be triggered again. This is called **spontaneous recovery**. In the Pavlov study of dogs if the bell was rung some time after the CR of salivation was extinct some saliva was produced. Spontaneous recovery does not always happen but depends on when and how the CS is presented following extinction.

Spontaneous recovery shows that extinction is not the 'forgetting' of the CR. Studies suggest that there are also other lasting effects of conditioning following extinction (Eichenbaum, 2008). One of these is the 'rapid reacquisition' of conditioned responses. This is the finding that, even after spontaneous recovery seems to have disappeared, it is easier to condition the same response again than to condition another animal. Another source of evidence that the CR is not lost during extinction is the occurrence of disinhibition. This is when a CR that seems to be extinct reappears in response to a different stimulus. For example, dogs may not salivate to the bell they were conditioned to but may salivate in response to another loud sound. These findings have led to the idea that extinction is not the forgetting of the CR but an inhibition of the CR.

Generalization and discrimination

Studies show a CR can be produced by stimuli that are similar to, but not identical to, the CS to which the animal had been conditioned. Pavlov called this phenomenon **stimulus generalization**. For example, if an animal is conditioned to salivate to one particular bell tone it may also respond to other tones that are similar to the original. Stimuli that are most similar to the original CS produce greater responses than stimuli that are less like the CS.

The opposite of stimulus generalization can also occur and animals can also learn to discriminate between different stimuli. This **stimulus discrimination** occurs during conditioning if one CS is paired with the UCS but others like it are not. For example, if dogs are given food (UCS) while one particular bell is rung (the CS) but when other similar bells are rung they are not given food. The dogs then show stimulus discrimination: they respond to one bell tone.

Timing of CS and UCS

The description of Pavlov's study suggests that, during conditioning, the UCS and the CS were always presented together. However, there are a number of ways of pairing the two stimuli, and the timing of the pairing of the CS and the UCS is important in the development of any CR. Eichenbaum (2008) suggests that there are four important variations in the timing between the UCS and CS:

1 *Delay conditioning*. In this type of conditioning the CS is presented for a fixed time period before the UCS is presented. The presentation of the UCS is delayed until the last part of the period and both end at the same time. This typically results in strong conditioning but the amount of conditioning decreases if the delay between CS and UCS onset becomes too large (Bouton, 2007).
2 *Trace conditioning.* In this type of conditioning the CS is again presented before the UCS but ends before the UCS starts. This also results in strong conditioning but the effects are weaker the longer the delay between the presentation of the CS and UCS.
3 *Simultaneous conditioning.* In this type of conditioning the CS and UCS are presented at the same time (that is, they begin and end at the same time). Intuitively this might seem like the best way of associating the CS and UCS but in practice it tends to produce weak conditioning.
4 *Backward conditioning.* In this type of conditioning the UCS is presented before the CS and ends before the UCS starts. This might result in some responses but usually produces very weak conditioning.

Type of conditioning	Description	Effect of conditioning
Delay	The CS precedes the UCS and overlaps with it.	Tends to result in the strongest conditioning.
Trace	The CS precedes the UCS and stops before the UCS begins.	Tends to result in strong conditioning.
Simultaneous	The CS and the UCS start and stop at the same time.	Tends to result in weak or no conditioning.
Backward	The CS is presented after the UCS.	Tends not to produce much conditioning.

Table 2.1 Variations in timing of the CS and UCS

Classical conditioning of emotional responses

The examples of classical conditioning discussed so far (salivating to the sound of a bell and blinking to the sound of a tone) have been based on simple reflex actions. However, there is evidence both from human and non-human animal studies that emotional responses can also be conditioned. An infamous example of this was the conditioning of a fear response in a human infant by Watson and Rayner (1920). They conditioned the infant, called Albert, to be afraid of a white rat. At the beginning of the study they established that Albert showed no particular fear response to the white rat (that is, it was a neutral stimulus) or to a wide range of other objects. However, Albert did show signs of fear when startled by a loud noise (a steel bar hit with a hammer). The loud noise was a UCS that produced a UCR of fear. During the conditioning every time Albert reached towards the white rat the researchers made the loud noise. After pairing the two stimuli together a few times the white rat alone caused fear. The white rat was a CS that produced a CS of fear.

Modern studies tend to use more sophisticated procedures and measures of emotion such as galvanic skin response (GSR) in humans or the conditioned emotional response technique in animals. In the conditioned emotional response studies non-human animals are conditioned using a light or a tone as a CS and a mild electric shock as an UCS. After CS has been paired with the shock several times the appearance of the CS suppresses other behaviour and may even cause 'freezing' in the animals. The suppression of other behaviour and freezing has been used as a measure of fear. These studies, like Watson and Rayner's, show that emotional responses (particularly fear) can be conditioned.

Explanations of classical conditioning

The discussion of classical conditioning so far has focused on *what* happens rather than *why* it happens. What is it that changes a previously neutral stimulus into a conditioned stimulus that causes a conditioned response? One of the early theories was that simply pairing two stimuli together is enough to cause an association or link between them. This is known as the principle of contiguity (Guthrie, 1935). Two types of evidence suggest this is incorrect. Firstly, as noted above, the timing of the CS and UCS is very important in determining whether a CR is produced. If the CS precedes the UCS (trace conditioning) conditioning tends to be strong. On the other hand if the UCS precedes the CS (backward conditioning) then conditioning often fails to take place. In both trace and backward conditioning there is a similar contiguity of stimuli, but one works and the other does not. A second problem for the principle of contiguity is the phenomena of **blocking**. This was shown by Kamin (1969) by using two groups of animals. The experimental group was initially conditioned by pairing a noise with an electric shock. A control group was not conditioned to respond to the noise. In the second stage of the study both groups received the same number of pairings of a compound stimulus of a light and noise with an electric shock. Finally the responses of both groups to the light alone were tested. Since both groups had the same number of pairings of the light with the electric shock the contiguity is the same. However, although the control group showed a strong conditioned response to the light the experimental group did not. The conditioning with the noise alone seemed to block further conditioning to the compound stimulus.

Rescorla and Wagner (1972) proposed a model of classical conditioning that seems to explain both the lack of effectiveness of backward conditioning and blocking. The details of the model are complex but the core concept is surprise. Learning is all about new stimuli or new situations, when things are no longer new, or surprising, learning stops (Bouton, 2007). When a CS is initially paired with a UCS it is surprising and learning takes place. This keeps happening over a number of trials but the amount of learning (measured by conditioning strength) decreases each time. Eventually conditioning strength is not increased by more trials. The association between the CS and the UCS stops being surprising. The CS now helps the animal predict the UCS.

The Rescorla-Wagner model provides a simple explanation of blocking. The experimental group had been conditioned with a noise paired with an electric shock. Eventually the noise came to predict the electric shock and learning stopped. When these animals were then exposed to the compound stimulus of a noise and a light paired with the shock the noise already predicted the shock. There was no surprise therefore no learning took place. This group failed to respond to the light alone. However, the control group had no previous training with either the noise or the light. When the compound stimulus was paired with the electric shock neither stimuli predicted the shock so it was a surprise. The group did learn and were conditioned to respond to the light. The notion of the CS predicting the UCS also explains the problem with some forms of conditioning. In both delay and trace conditioning the CS precedes the UCS. At first this is surprising but eventually the association between the two is learned. In backward conditioning the UCS precedes the CS. Although the UCS will be a surprise since the CS follows the UCS it cannot be used to predict the UCS. No association is formed.

The Rescorla-Wagner model is a very influential model that is useful in helping to understand some of the experimental findings about classical conditioning. However, some of the assumptions of the model have been challenged. For example, the explanation for the failure of conditioning with the compound stimulus in blocking experiments is lack of surprise. Other researchers have questioned this assumption and have examined the role of attention (Pearce, 2008). It may be possible that animals do not respond to the second stimulus because they do not pay attention to it. In the Kamin experiment, animals may have not attended to the light since they had already learned that the noise was an important stimulus.

Evaluation of the role of classical conditioning in the behaviour of animals

Classical conditioning is able to explain how one simple form of learning takes place. It shows how animals, including humans, can learn to react to new stimuli. Classical conditioning can be useful in foraging and diet selection. Some potential food sources can be harmful. Learning which sources are harmful helps animals survive. Garcia and Koelling (1966) showed that classical conditioning causes some animals to avoid food that made them ill. They carried out a series of studies of taste aversion and found that pairing novel tasting water with an emetic (a substance that causes vomiting) was enough to make rats avoid the taste in the future. They found that even if the rats were ill up to six hours after tasting the water they still learned to avoid the taste that was linked to the illness. Rats are omnivores that forage for a variety of food sources: it makes sense to avoid those tastes that make them ill. Garcia, Rusiniak and Brett (1977) showed that taste aversion can also happen in the wild. They fed coyotes mutton wrapped in sheep hide that was laced with an emetic. This made the coyotes ill. Later, when given the opportunity to attack sheep the coyotes turned away; they had developed an aversion. Taste aversion can happen in humans as well. Food that is associated with illness can become unpalatable or produce feelings of nausea. For example, a friend once ate many olives before succumbing to a very unpleasant stomach bug. Although she used to enjoy olives, the thought of them now makes her feel ill. Classical conditioning may also enable animals to associate fear with a new stimulus if it is paired with a predator. The linking of emotional responses to stimuli can help survival.

However, classical conditioning does have some limitations. Firstly, it is not clear if any study of classical conditioning of one behaviour in one species can be generalized to either other behaviours or other species. Seligman (1970) points out that animals have evolved to survive in different environments and situations. In order to adapt to a particular environment some animals might learn some things more easily than others. Therefore animals may be prepared to learn some associations but not others. Seligman called this concept 'preparedness'. He notes for example that humans seem 'prepared' to learn to fear spiders and snakes more than other objects. The concept of preparedness also extends to studies of taste aversion. Garcia and Koelling (1966) found that pairing a taste with nausea conditioned animals to avoid the taste in future. However, pairing an audiovisual stimulus ('bright-noisy water') with nausea did not lead to avoidance of the bright-noisy water. Rats are 'prepared' to learn to avoid tastes that make them ill but not to avoid audiovisual stimuli.

Classical conditioning is limited in explaining learning in animals. Classical conditioning only links an existing response to a new stimulus. Animals do not learn new behaviours by classical conditioning. Conditioning dogs to salivate to a bell does not teach a new response, just the same response to new stimulus. However, it is clear that animals do learn new behaviours in order to adapt to their environment. For example, pets that are in the unnatural environment of a house can learn to adapt to it. Some cats learn to jump and pull door handles to open doors. This is not based on an existing 'door opening' reflex but is a new behaviour. It is even more important for animals to learn new behaviours in natural settings since it affects their chance of survival. Animals have to learn new behaviours to get food, avoid predators and so on. Classical conditioning does not explain how these new behaviours can be learned.

Thinking scientifically → **Validation of new knowledge**

New scientific knowledge is validated by a process known as peer review. Before new work is published it is sent for review by independent experts (the peers). They check the background information, examine the method used and assess the findings and conclusions. This is designed to act as a form of quality control and ensures only good research is entered into the public domain. However, this process can be slow and sometimes can even stop publication of new knowledge. For example, Garcia and Koelling (1966) found that rats could be conditioned to avoid flavoured water even when there was a large gap between tasting the water and being ill. The reviewers of this work initially found this hard to believe and rejected the work for publication. All other classical conditioning work up to this point suggested that a conditioned response could not be learned if the gap between the conditioned stimulus and the unconditioned response was more than a few minutes. However, Garcia and Koelling found rats developed taste aversions even when there was a six-hour gap between tasting the water (CS) and being ill (UCR). As a result, the publication of their work was delayed until other researchers began to notice the same effect.

Even though peer review is a good process for validating new knowledge it does have some problems. It tends to be a conservative process that is cautious about accepting new ideas. In Kuhn's (1996) view of science, peer review can prolong periods of 'normal science' and delay 'revolution'.

Summary

Classical conditioning occurs when a stimulus that naturally triggers a response is paired with another neutral stimulus. The neutral stimulus becomes a learned, or conditioned, stimulus that triggers the same response which is now called a conditioned response. Many responses can be conditioned in this way including salivation, blinking and emotional reactions such as fear. Conditioned responses become extinct if the conditioned stimulus is presented repeatedly without the unconditioned stimulus. However, the response is not forgotten since it can reappear (spontaneous recovery) and is easier to recondition in the future. Conditioned responses also show generalization and discrimination. Generalization occurs when stimuli that are similar to the conditioned stimulus also cause the conditioned response. Discrimination occurs when the conditioned response occurs only in response to a narrow range of stimuli.

There have been a number of theories of how classical conditioning works. The contiguity theory suggests that a neutral stimulus becomes a conditioned stimulus because it is closely associated with the unconditioned stimulus. However, this fails to explain why backward conditioning is ineffective, or the phenomenon of blocking. The Rescorla–Wagner model suggests that surprise plays a part in learning. At first the conditioned stimulus fails to predict the occurrence of the unconditioned stimulus and the association between the two becomes learned. This explains why backward conditioning fails. There is a question about whether conditioning is best explained by the concept of surprise or attention.

Classical conditioning can explain how animals learn to react to new stimuli and is helpful in explaining behaviours such as diet selection and avoidance of predators. However, theories of classical conditioning do not explain why animals seem to be prepared to learn some responses but not others. Classical conditioning also fails to explain how animals learn new behaviour.

Operant conditioning

Classical conditioning provides a good explanation of how animals may learn to respond to a new stimulus but does not explain how animals learn new behaviours. Pavlov's dogs learned to salivate to the sound of a bell but salivation was not a new behaviour. Yet animals learn more than just responses to new stimuli; they learn new behaviours to adapt to their environment. For example, there is a squirrel in my garden that learned to climb a pole to get at seeds I put out for birds. I changed the position of the seed feeder and put it on a line. Within a few days the squirrel had adapted its behaviour and would climb a post and then go upside down along the line to the seed feeder. This illustrates a type of learning described by Skinner (1938) which he called operant conditioning. He called it operant because the animal is operating on the environment. Skinner found that this operant behaviour is affected by the consequences of the behaviour. Skinner studied how animals learn by the rewards or punishments they get following behaviour. The squirrel in my garden learns new behaviour to get seed rewards.

Skinner's work on operant conditioning built on earlier work by Thorndike (1911). Thorndike did a variety of studies to investigate how animals solved problems. For example, in one study he observed how cats learned to escape from a puzzle box he devised. The cats were put inside the box and some food was placed outside. To escape from the box the cats had to learn to operate a latch. When a cat was placed in the box for the first occasion it took some time before they released the catch. However, after being placed in the box a number of times (a number of 'trials') they became faster and faster until eventually the cat would release the catch immediately it was put inside the box. This type of learning is called trial and error learning (the more trials, the fewer errors). This and other studies led to Thorndike's law of (positive) effect which states that any behaviour that is followed by a pleasurable outcome is more likely to be repeated.

Skinner built on Thorndike's work but studied behaviour in a more controlled and scientific way using apparatus now known as Skinner boxes. These vary in design for different animals but all have a very plain environment that eliminates extraneous variables (that is, a controlled environment). Typically they include only a device to measure behaviour (such as a lever rats could push or a disk pigeons could peck at) and a means of delivering some food. In one version of the Skinner box rats were taught to press a lever. When the rats were first put into the box they moved around in it. As they explored the box they eventually pressed the lever by accident. This accidental behaviour was rewarded with a food pellet. After this happened a few times the rats began to press the lever more and more often. The behaviour became a learned response encouraged by the food reward. Skinner called the food, and anything else that made behaviour more likely to happen again, a **reinforcer**. He found that learning a new behaviour was determined by whether it was reinforced or not. In the Skinner box the food acted as **reinforcement** for the lever pressing.

The Skinner box is a controlled environment that allows the activity of the animals to be recorded automatically. This allowed Skinner to study the learning of responses precisely and accurately. He found that operant conditioning depended on the relationships between A-B-C. The initials ABC stand for antecedents (the stimulus conditions before the behaviour, for example the box and lever), behaviours (what the animal does, that is, presses the lever) and consequences (what happens after the behaviour, that is, given reinforcement) (see Figures 2.3 and 2.4).

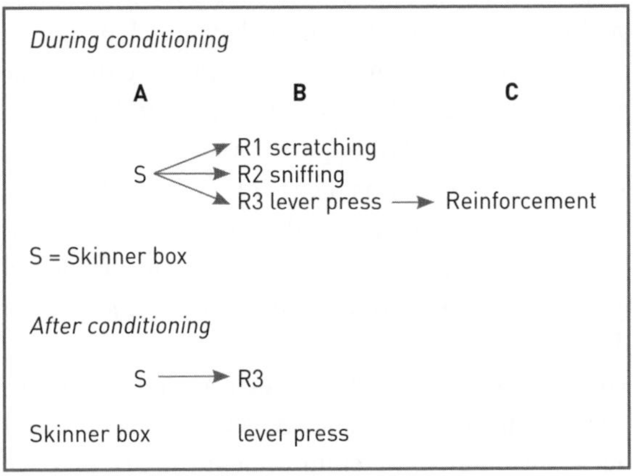

Figure 2.3 General process of operant conditioning

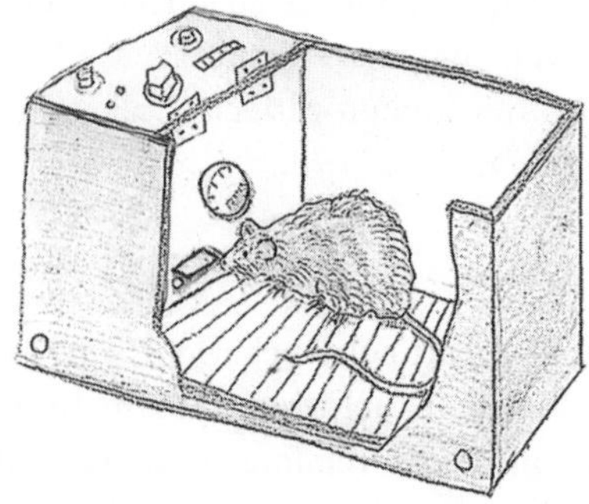

Figure 2.4 The Skinner Box Stimulation can be presented via electrified grid, speakers and lights. Rats respond by pressing a lever. (Illustration: Bryony Budd)

Skinner showed that the learning of new, voluntary behaviour is governed by the consequences of the behaviour. He also showed that subtle changes in the way reinforcement was given had profound effects on behaviour (see schedules of reinforcement below).

Skinner also found that there were individual differences in how the animals learned using operant conditioning. Reinforcement was given after the required behaviour such as pressing a lever. However, each animal learned to press the lever in their own way, some used the right paw, others used the left and a few used their nose. This illustrates an important distinction between classical and operant conditioning. In classical conditioning a conditioned response is elicited by a stimulus and, although this response can vary in intensity, it does not vary in the behaviour shown. In operant conditioning behaviour depends on the consequences of the behaviour and thus it can potentially be anything. For example, in one study Skinner put pigeons in boxes and gave then food at regular intervals. Although the food was not given for any particular behaviour most birds behaved as if it did. One pigeon learned to rock its head back and forth while another turned counterclockwise. Skinner called these behaviours that developed from accidental pairing of behaviour and reinforcement, *superstitious behaviour* (Skinner, 1948).

As with classical conditioning, behaviours learned by operant conditioning show both extinction and spontaneous recovery. In operant conditioning behaviour is maintained by reinforcement (that is, rats will continue to press levers if the behaviour is followed by food). If the reinforcement is removed animals stop exhibiting the behaviour (that is, the rats will sooner or later stop pressing the lever if food is no longer given). Behaviour that appears to be extinct can sometimes reappear at a later time without giving any reinforcement. In common with classical conditioning, this is called spontaneous recovery.

Schedules of reinforcement

When animals are conditioned to show a particular behaviour, such as pressing a bar, they are given reinforcement each time they make an appropriate response. This is called continuous reinforcement. One of the important features of operant conditioning is that, once a behaviour is learned, it does not need continuous reinforcement. In most studies reinforcement is given on an intermittent schedule where responses are only reinforced occasionally. Skinner found that changing the schedule in which reinforcement is given changes the ways animals respond. When he gave reinforcement less frequently it changed both the response rate (that is, how often a rat presses a lever) and the extinction rate (that is, how long the rat continues to press the lever once reinforcement is no longer given).

Apart from continuous reinforcement there are four other types of schedule that use partial reinforcement. Partial schedules are arranged on either a ratio or an interval basis. Ratio schedules are based on delivering reinforcement based on the number of responses an animal makes. In a fixed ratio schedule, reinforcement is given after a fixed number of responses. For example, on a fixed ratio schedule of 25 a rat would need to press a lever 25 times after the last reinforcement before it received reinforcement again. In a variable ratio schedule, reinforcement is given after a changeable number of responses with the number of responses set around an average ratio. For example, on a variable ratio schedule of 25 a rat might get a reinforcement after pressing the lever 15 times on one occasion but the next after 35 times. The exact number of responses may change each time but the average would be 25.

Interval schedules are based on the time that has elapsed since the last reinforcement was given. In a fixed interval schedule, reinforcement is given after the first response after a fixed period of time. For example, on a fixed interval schedule of 60 seconds a rat would be given reinforcement the first time it pressed the lever after 60 seconds following the last reinforcement. Any responses before the 60-second interval would not be reinforced. In a variable interval schedule, reinforcement is given after a changeable time period set around an average time. For example, on a variable interval schedule of 60 seconds a rat might be reinforced for the first response after 80 seconds on one occasion but after 40 on another.

Each schedule results in a distinct pattern of behaviour and a different resistance to extinction (see Table 2.2). Generally the response rate is higher in the ratio schedules than the interval schedules. In a fixed ratio schedule there a usually a lull in responses after a reinforcement (known as the postreinforcement pause); this is followed by a rapid response rate. Similarly in a fixed ratio schedule there is slow rate of response following a reinforcement followed by a rapid response rate towards the end of the interval. Both variable schedules show a steady rate of responding but the ratio schedule produces a higher response rate. Fixed schedules (whether ratio or interval) show a fast extinction rate when reinforcement ceases. Both variable schedules are associated with slow extinction rates.

These schedules might seem rather theoretical and inconsequential at first sight. However, they have a large impact on the behaviour of animals, including humans. For example, one behaviour that can become a problem for some people is gambling. Gamblers tend to get reinforced on a variable ratio schedule (they might win after one bet but then not win again until after ten bets). Many gamblers have a compulsion to bet (a high response rate) and find it difficult to stop gambling (a slow extinction rate). This is predicted by the behaviour of rats in a Skinner box!

Schedule of reinforcement	Description	Effect on response	Effect on extinction
Continuous reinforcement	Reinforcement follows every single appropriate response.	Response rate is low but regular.	Extinction is very rapid.
Fixed ratio (FR)	A reinforcement is given after a fixed number of responses.	Response rate is high. There tends to be a lull after each reinforcement, followed by rapid responding.	Extinction is fast.
Variable ratio (VR)	A reinforcement is given after a number of responses but that number varies each time around an average value.	Response rate is high and steady.	Extinction is slow. VR tends to be the most resistant to extinction.
Fixed interval (FI)	A reinforcement is given after a fixed period provided the response is made at least once during the period.	Response rate is low. There is a pause after each reinforcement with an increase in responding towards the end of an interval.	Extinction is fast.
Variable interval (VI)	A reinforcement is given after periods that vary around an average time provided the response is made at least once during any period.	Response rate is moderate. The pattern is fairly steady but there is some increase in responding as the time since the last reinforcement increases.	Extinction is slow.

Table 2.2 Schedules of reinforcement

Positive and negative reinforcement

When Skinner conditioned rats to press a lever by reinforcing them with food he was using one particular form of reinforcement called **positive reinforcement**. Positive reinforcement occurs when a behaviour is followed by a reward or some kind of pleasurable stimulus. Behaviour followed by a positive reinforcement is more likely to be repeated in the future. Many things can act as a positive reinforcer such as food to a hungry animal or water to a thirsty animal. An alternative means of conditioning is to use **negative reinforcement**. Negative reinforcement involves the removal of or avoidance of an aversive or unpleasant stimulus. For example, if an animal is conditioned to turn off a loud noise by pushing a lever the removal of the loud noise acts a negative reinforcement. Both positive and negative reinforcement strengthen behaviour and both make behaviour more likely to occur in the future. Negative reinforcement should not be confused with **punishment**. Punishment is the presentation of an unpleasant stimulus after a behaviour. This weakens behaviour and makes it less likely to happen in the future. For example, if after pressing a lever a rat is subjected to a loud unpleasant noise it makes lever pressing less likely to happen again in the future. The loud noise acts as a punishment.

The role of negative reinforcement in learning can be studied using a modified version of the Skinner box called a shuttle box. A shuttle box consists of two compartments that are separated by a barrier or an opening. Typically each side has a metal grid floor that can be used to deliver a mild electric shock. There is also some means of delivering a warning stimulus such as a light or a tone. In *escape learning* a rat is placed on one side of the box and an electric current is applied to the grid in that side. The rat may show a variety of behaviours but eventually will move to the other side of the box where there is no current. After a number of trials the rats become conditioned to go to the other side as soon as the current starts. This demonstrates how negative reinforcement can be used to condition behaviour.

In *avoidance learning* there is a warning stimulus before the current starts. Again rats learn to escape from the electric current by going to the other side. However in this situation the rats learn to go to the other side as soon as the warning signal is given (that is, before the electric current begins). They learn to avoid the unpleasant stimuli. Roberts (1998) suggests that avoidance learning raises an apparent paradox. When the animals learn to go from one side of the box when the warning stimulus occurs there is no consequence to their behaviour (that is, they are not stopping an unpleasant stimulus because they avoid it). He suggests that this paradox can be explained by a two-factor theory of avoidance learning. This proposes that in the early stage of avoidance learning rats learn to fear the warning stimulus through classical conditioning. They then learn to reduce this fear by moving to the other side of the box by operant conditioning (the consequence of moving is to reduce the unpleasant feeling of fear).

Primary and secondary reinforcement

All the positive and negative reinforcers described so far have been primary. **Primary reinforcers** are stimuli that reinforce behaviour naturally and satisfy a biological need. These include food, water, sex and avoidance of pain. They are also known as unconditioned reinforcers since they are not learned but innate. A **secondary reinforcer** on the other hand does not act as a reinforcer naturally but is initially a neutral stimulus. However if this neutral stimulus is paired with a primary reinforcer enough times it begins to act as a reinforcer itself. For example, a tone does not act as a reinforcer for rats. However, if rats are given food (a primary reinforcer) and hear a tone each time they press a lever the tone will eventually become a secondary reinforcer. This can be shown by the lack of extinction when the food is stopped. Rats continue to press the lever because the tone acts as a secondary reinforcer. Secondary reinforcers are also known as conditioned reinforcers because they are learned.

A good example of secondary reinforcement comes from a study involving the 'chimp-o-mat' (Wolfe, 1936). In this study chimpanzees were trained to pull a heavy lever to get plastic tokens. The plastic tokens were not a positive reinforcement at first but could be exchanged for grapes in the chimp-o-mat. However, eventually the plastic tokens seemed to become a secondary reinforcer and several of the chimpanzees built up a hoard of tokens. Humans also tend to hoard a form of token, money. Money can be exchanged for food, drink, and so on but for many people it acquires value itself; it becomes a secondary reinforcer.

Behaviour shaping

In operant conditioning animals learning a behaviour depends on the consequences of the behaviour. This is easy to understand when considering a simple behaviour, such as pressing a lever, which might occur by chance but does not seem to explain learning of complex behaviour. The likelihood of a complete complex behaviour occurring by chance that is then followed by reinforcement seems remote. For example, Skinner once taught pigeons to play ping-pong. The chances of two pigeons spontaneously knocking a ball back and forth over a table are extremely low. So how could Skinner reinforce this behaviour? The answer is by **behaviour shaping** or successive approximations.

This is the process of giving reinforcement for behaviour that gradually becomes more and more like the complex behaviour desired. In the case of the pigeons they were first reinforced for pecking near the ball, then to tap the ball, then to knock the ball on the ping-pong table and so on. Using behaviour shaping, animals can be taught complex sequences of actions. All the complex animal behaviour sequences seen in films are taught using this technique.

Bouton (2007) describes how behaviour shaping might work in natural settings and cites the behaviour of crows on a beach in British Columbia. At low tide the crows pick up the largest whelks they can find then fly about five metres above some rocks and drop them. This cracks open the shells and allows the crows to eat them. Bouton suggests that this complex behaviour may be shaped. For example, at first crows might dig among the whelks and find one that had been cracked open by the tide and eat it. This would reinforce digging behaviour. This increases the likelihood that whelks are lifted and dropped. If this leads to further cracking of shells it causes further reinforcement. The behaviour of the crow becomes shaped.

Evaluation of the role of operant conditioning in the behaviour of animals

Many animals need to learn new behaviour in order to survive in a complex environment. They need to find food sources, find or build shelter and to avoid threats. Operant conditioning provides an explanation of how animals learn new behaviour because of the consequence of the behaviour. Behaviour that is reinforced tends to be repeated but behaviour that is punished is not. Thus operant conditioning demonstrates how reinforcement and punishment in the animal's past shape and guide future behaviour. A bird that is reinforced with food when it lands on a bird table is likely to land there again. It can also explain how animals learn complex sequences of behaviour through behaviour shaping. For example, if the source of food is progressively changed in a garden, squirrels will learn an elaborate 'routine' to get the food.

Although operant conditioning provides a good explanation of learning new behaviour, there are some problems with the theory.

Operant conditioning explains learning by showing how stimuli and responses are linked. This ignores the effect of any intervening factors such as thinking (or cognition). However, there is evidence to suggest that these intervening, cognitive factors are important in animal learning. There is evidence that some animals can solve problems by thinking about them rather than receiving reinforcement in a trial and error fashion (see studies of insight in 'Problems of simple learning theories' below).

A second problem is that traditional operant conditioning theory tends to ignore animals' evolutionary history (that is, an assumption that all learning using positive or negative reinforcement is the same). However, there is a lot of evidence that some behaviours are learned much more easily than others. For instance, Bolles (1972) found that it is much easier to teach a rat to jump from a box to avoid a shock than go from one side to another in a shuttle box. It is very difficult to teach rats to avoid a shock by pressing a lever. He suggests that this is because each species has evolved behaviours he called 'species-specific defence reactions'. In natural conditions, jumping out of the way to avoid an unpleasant stimulus would be an effective response but pushing a lever would not.

Bouton (2007) suggests that Skinner's work on operant conditioning describes the relationship between behaviour and its consequence but does not explain how or why it happens. Thus it is a description of what happens rather than a theory of learning. It does not explain how or why reinforcers strengthen behaviour. Bouton further suggests that Skinner's definition of reinforcers is circular. A reinforcer is something that strengthens behaviour. If we then ask why does it strengthen behaviour the answer is, because it is a reinforcer.

Another problem is that not all reinforcers have the same effect, and may have different effects depending on the state of an animal. Food will strengthen a behaviour in a very hungry animal much more than in a well fed animal. Furthermore, as Bouton (2007, p. 250) notes, 'reinforcers are not all alike. Although they have similar effects ... they do not necessarily substitute for one another'. Thus although 'food' is a positive reinforcer I suspect chocolate would be a more effective reinforcer than sprouts in children's learning! Eysenck (2004) points out that Skinner tended to exaggerate the importance of external factors (such as reinforcement) and minimized the importance of internal factors (such as motivation).

Thinking scientifically → **Behaviourism and science**

The types of learning discussed in this chapter, classical and operant conditioning, are associated with the behaviourist approach to psychology. Skinner, the most famous radical behaviourist, argued that psychologists should take a strictly scientific approach to the study of behaviour and that they should only study what can be observed. For behaviourists, psychology is the study of behaviour, it is not the study of the mind. We can observe stimuli and responses to the stimuli but the intervening processes (mental activities or the mind) are in a black box into which we cannot see.

This ignores a lot of human experience. As I write this I am thinking, as you read it you are thinking. As I have written this chapter I have experienced a number of emotions (chiefly irritation and anxiety but some happiness!). These factors play an important part in our lives and in our learning and so researchers began to question the relevance of the behaviourist approach. This is evident in the 'cognitive revolution' of the 1970s when researchers began to probe the black box. Cognitive psychologists also looked at stimuli and responses but did so to try to understand how mental processes worked (how do we take in the information about stimuli, how do we store it, how do we manipulate it in order to respond and so on).

Skinner however maintained that behaviourism was the only way for psychology to progress. In an article called 'Why I am not a cognitive psychologist' (1977) he notes, 'I am not a cognitive psychologist for several reasons. I see no evidence of an inner world of mental life relative either to an analysis of behavior as a function of environmental forces or to the physiology of the nervous system'.

Summary

Operant conditioning demonstrates how the learning of new behaviour is contingent on the consequences of the behaviour. Behaviour that is followed by reinforcement gets strengthened and repeated. Reinforcement does not need to follow each behaviour, and varying in the way reinforcement is given (schedules of reinforcement) alters both the response and extinction rates of behaviour. Reinforcement can be positive (presentation of a pleasant stimulus) or negative (removal of an unpleasant stimulus). Some reinforcers (such as food, water and the avoidance of pain) seem to be innate and are called primary reinforcers.

Other stimuli can become reinforcers through their association with primary reinforcers; these are known as secondary reinforcers. Operant conditioning can also show how animals learn complex sequences of actions through behaviour shaping. It provides a powerful explanation of how animals learn new behaviour.

The focus of operant conditioning is on learning of responses because of the consequence of the response. It assumes all learning can be explained by examining the antecedents, the behaviour and the consequences. This ignores a number of other factors that affect learning. Firstly, it does not take the evolutionary history of animals into account. However, studies have shown that some behaviours, such as species-specific defence reactions, seem to be based on biology not consequences of the behaviour. Secondly, operant conditioning theory ignores the role of cognition (information processing) in learning. However, there is evidence that not all behaviour is learned by operant conditioning and that some animal learning indicates that cognitive factors are involved.

Problems of simple learning theories

The ability to learn to respond to new stimuli or to learn a new behaviour is biologically important. Animals need to adapt to their environment and change behaviour to meet the challenge of new circumstances. Classical conditioning is able to explain how animals, including humans, can learn to react to new stimuli. However, it not clear that studies of classical conditioning can be generalized. Also classical conditioning is limited in its explanation of learning in animals as it fails to explain how they learn new behaviour. Operant conditioning explains how animals learn new and potentially complex behaviour and how behaviour can be shaped by its consequences.

Nevertheless, classical conditioning and operant conditioning do not explain all learning in animals. These explanations of learning concentrate on the links between stimuli and responses and ignore the effect of other factors. Cognitive, or information processing, theories emphasize the role of thinking (cognition) between stimuli and response. There is evidence to suggest that these intervening, cognitive factors are important in animal learning. In one series of studies, Kohler (1925) gave chimpanzees problems to solve. However, unlike Thorndike's study of cats, he did not find that the chimpanzees solved the problems using trial and error. He found that they often showed the solution to the problem after a period of inactivity. In other words the chimpanzees seemed to solve the problem by using a mental representation of it. Kohler called this **insight learning**. In one example, a chimpanzee was in a cage and some fruit was left outside the cage beyond the reach of the chimpanzee. Kohler left a short stick inside the cage but this was too short to reach the fruit. There was a longer stick outside the cage that could reach the fruit but this was just out of reach for the chimpanzee. Initially the chimpanzee tried to get fruit with the short stick but then gave up. After gazing at the fruit for a while the chimpanzee suddenly picked up the short stick and used it to get the long stick. He then immediately used the long stick to get the fruit. Kohler believes this shows learning by insight. The chimpanzee had solved the problem by thinking about it. However, Pearce (2008) points out that there is a problem with this explanation. The apparent lack of trial and error may be due to prior practice of using sticks to gain reward in the past (that is, the trial and error learning occurred before the study).

There is also evidence of learning in the absence of reinforcement. In one experiment Tolman and Honzik (1930) allowed one group of rats to wander in a complicated maze with no reinforcement, but reinforced another group when they reached the goal point. As predicted by operant conditioning, the rats in the reinforced group soon learned to run to the end of the maze but the rats in the first group did not. The non-reinforced group was given reinforcement on the 11th trial. This group learned to reach the end much quicker than the group that had been reinforced from the beginning. By trial 12, the non-reinforced group reached the goal point as quickly as the reinforced group (that is, they achieved the same performance with 1 reinforcement as the reinforced group did with 11). This suggests that the non-reinforced group had been learning about the maze in the first 10 trials but did not show this learning (Bouton, 2007). This experiment shows **latent learning** in animals and demonstrates the distinction between learning and performance. The non-reinforced group had been learning but it did not show in their performance. However, as soon as reinforcement was introduced the rats demonstrated that they had learned a route through the maze. Conditioning may be a better predictor of performance rather than learning.

Conditioning theories also fail to explain learning by imitation or observation. Conditioning theories suggest that learning occurs because of reinforcement of the individual animal. However studies of social learning (see Chapter 3) show that animals can learn by imitating others without reinforcement. For instance, Marshall-Pescini and Whiten (2008) investigated the use of tools to crack nuts in chimpanzees. This is a skill restricted to some groups only but they found it could be acquired by social learning in a group of sanctuary-living chimpanzees.

Further reading

Bouton, M.E. (2007) *Learning and Behaviour: A Contemporary Synthesis*. Sunderland, MA: Sinauer Associates.

Eichenbaum, H. (2008) *Learning and Memory*. New York, NY: W.W. Norton & Company.

Chapter 3

Animal intelligence

This chapter is about intelligence in non-human animals. The discussion of 'what is intelligence' in Chapter 1 should have demonstrated that the concept of intelligence is difficult to define. When this concept is applied to non-human animals, it becomes even more difficult to define, partly because of the problem of assessing non-human intelligence. As Byrne and Bates (2007, p. 715) note 'comparative psychology has found no acceptable "intelligence" test for animals'. Nevertheless Pearce (2008) discuses three characteristics that may be used to define and assess animal intelligence: adaptability, learning and information processing. He notes that few would disagree that adaptability of behaviour is a sign of intelligence, but points out that it is difficult to identify the mechanisms that enable an animal to adapt (that is, is it an adaptation caused by evolution or the individual's response to the environment?). He suggests therefore, that the capacity to learn to adapt and the ability to process information are better indications of intelligence. In the previous chapter, the role of associative learning in enabling animals to adapt was considered. These explanations concentrate on the learning and adaptability of individuals. However, there are many other types of evidence of intelligence in non-human animals including social learning, Machiavellian intelligence, theory of mind, self-recognition and metacognition. This type of evidence, based on the processing of social information, is discussed in this chapter. A different source of evidence of intelligence, the possibility that animals might be capable of using language, is discussed in the next chapter.

This chapter will cover:

- Social learning
- Machiavellian intelligence

- Theory of mind
- Self-recognition
- Metacognition
- Comparisons of intelligence in non-human animals

Social learning

Many animals live in social groups and have the potential to be influenced by others. It is possible that some new behaviour is not the result of individual learning but of social learning. Animals might learn by observing others of the same species and imitating behaviour rather than learning from the potentially dangerous process of trial and error. Pearce (2008) has identified a number of ways that social learning could benefit animals. The solutions to some complex problems may be learned by imitating others. Social learning might help inform foraging behaviour and diet choice and thus help animals avoid poor or poisonous food. Copying other animals' reactions to predators may benefit both an individual animal and its social group. There seems to be evidence for each of these.

Problem solving using imitation

Animals are faced with a range of problems. For example, they may find a potentially rich food source that is protected in some way (for example a hard shell) and they face the problem of getting the food. Some problems are so difficult that they may not be solved in a lifetime of trial and error by individual animals. Nonetheless if the problem is solved by one individual, it would be very advantageous to the rest of the group if they could learn the solution. One mechanism for learning is imitation, where animals watch the behaviour of other animals and 'imitate' that behaviour.

Roberts (1998) suggests that there are several criteria that can be used to determine imitative behaviour. Firstly, the behaviour should be novel and complex and not part of an animal's natural repertoire. Secondly, it must be based on observation not the result of reinforcement. The third criterion is that the behaviour must be seen repeatedly. He also notes that evidence of true imitation is difficult to find from naturalistic studies.

This is partly because it is impossible to eliminate the possibility that the behaviour is not due to prior reinforcement.

An illustration of this is the rapid spread of tearing the foil on milk-bottle tops by blue tits and great tits in Britain (Hinde and Fisher, 1951). This behaviour was first noted in one location in the 1920s, but by the late 1940s it was observed throughout Britain. One explanation for the rapid spread of this behaviour is that the birds learned by imitation. It seemed difficult to account for the sudden appearance of the novel behaviour throughout a whole country in any other way.

However, laboratory studies have questioned whether the learning of the new behaviour was due to imitation. Sherry and Galef (1984) have shown that if a bird is exposed to an already opened bottle it will drink the milk. The bird is reinforced and is more likely to land on a bottle and then to open the foil itself in the future. The bird learns by reinforcement not imitation.

Another famous example that seems to provide better evidence of apparent imitation was seen in observations of monkeys. One troop of Japanese macaque monkeys on an island were observed over a period of time. In order to observe them easily the researcher left sweet potatoes on the beach (Kawai, 1965). During one observation a young female took a sweet potato to the sea and washed the mud off it. This was the first time this behaviour had been observed and she then repeated this behaviour on subsequent occasions (presumably because the potatoes tasted better). The researcher noticed that after a short time other monkeys also washed their potatoes. The behaviour became common in this particular troop of monkeys but it is not seen in other troops. One explanation of this is that the monkeys learned the behaviour by imitation.

Nagell, Olguin and Tomasello (1993) believe there is an alternative explanation which does not rely on imitation. They suggest that the practice may be spread through **stimulus enhancement**. In this case the observer monkeys may direct their behaviour to the stimulus of the sweet potato because of the activity of the monkey in the sea. If other monkeys then follow that monkey to the sea for social reasons they may learn by accident that the sea washes off the mud. This explanation may seem contrived, but it does have the advantage of explaining the spread of behaviour using established processes. It also helps explain why many of the monkeys who showed the potato washing behaviour after the first one were young. These are more likely to follow an experienced monkey for social reasons.

The imitation shown by a group of orang-utans in a camp in Indonesia is more difficult to explain by reinforcement (Russon and Galdikas, 1993). All the orang-utans were ex-captive animals that were being rehabilitated to live in a natural environment. They were free to roam freely through the camp and observed the humans in the camp engage in a variety of complex activities such as cooking and building. The camp workers observed that the orang-utans began to imitate some of these complex activities and recorded them in detail. These observations showed some behaviours that closely matched human activities and were so complex that they could not have been the result of prior reinforcement. Although stimulus enhancement might explain why the orang-utans' attention was drawn to the activities, it is difficult to see what could reinforce the imitative behaviour.

The problem with all naturalistic studies is that they are difficult to interpret. Experimental studies are able to provide better evidence since they help establish cause and effect. Whiten et al. (1996) carried out an experimental study of imitation in chimpanzees. Chimpanzees observed a human open an artificial fruit box. The box could only be opened by operating a bolt mechanism. One group of chimpanzees saw the human operate the bolt by twisting and pulling it but another group saw the human operate the bolt by poking it out. When the chimpanzees were given the opportunity to open the box each group used the technique they had observed. Roberts (1998) suggests that this shows precise imitation of observed behaviour that is difficult to explain by stimulus enhancement or social facilitation.

Nut cracking behaviour in wild chimpanzees seems to be restricted to a few groups. Marshall-Pescini and Whiten (2008) have investigated this behaviour with a group of sanctuary-living chimpanzees. They used an experimental method to test whether the behaviour could be learned by imitation. They found it could be acquired in a just few days by chimpanzees aged three to four or older. They believe their results are explained by social learning. There is also some evidence that mother chimpanzees teach the skill of cracking nuts to their juvenile offspring (Boesch, 1991). In order to crack the hard nuts successfully the animals need an appropriate hard surface (the anvil) and a rock of just the right weight (the hammer). The adult chimpanzees were seen to place nuts on the anvil and leave them for the juveniles to crack. The mothers were also observed giving good hammers to their offspring.

Imitation of diet

Some animals have a varied diet that requires the animal to learn to discriminate between good, poor and even dangerous food sources. Rats, for example, will eat nearly anything that is not poisonous and may have to learn about hundreds of food sources during their life. There is evidence that rats tend to go where others are feeding and thus are guided to safe food sources. Groups of rats with different potential food sources can have very different diets. Rats typically have a grain-based diet but it can be predominately trout (from a trout hatchery), sparrows and even molluscs (Galef, 1980). However, after a series of experiments on diving for molluscs, Galef concluded that much of the difference in rat diet could be explained by 'natural shaping' rather than social learning. This natural shaping comes from differences in food distribution, which results in a behaviour shaping procedure that occurs in nature. If a rat's main food source is at the bottom of a stream then the environment, not other rats, shapes the behaviour of the animal. Better evidence for social learning of diet in the wild comes from a field study of immature orang-utans (Jaeggi et al., 2009). This found that the immature orang-utans rarely foraged independently but selectively observed their mothers. The diets of the immature orang-utans were identical to their mothers even though the diets of each mother differed. Jaeggi et al. refer to this as the 'vertical transmission' of diet choice and note that a number of complex foraging behaviours seemed to be learned by observation.

There is also experimental evidence that social learning can influence foraging behaviour. In a study of Burmese jungle fowl, one group of fowl learned which one of four bowls in an enclosure contained food and went to it consistently (McQuoid and Galef, 1992). The behaviour of this group can be explained by operant conditioning (they received reinforcement when they went to this bowl). A second group (the observers) was allowed to watch the first group walk into the enclosure and then feed from the food-containing bowl. When the observers were released into the enclosure they showed a preference for going to the food bowl. McQuoid and Galef (1992) suggest this is due to stimulus enhancement. The stimulus (bowl) has been enhanced because the observer's attention was drawn to it.

There is evidence that rats can acquire a preference for a particular food from other rats even if they do not see the others eat it. In studies by Galef (1988) rats were put in pairs and one of the pair (the demonstrator) was placed in isolation and then fed a distinctive flavoured food (either cocoa or cinnamon). The demonstrator rat was then put back with the other rat (the observer) for 30 minutes without any food. Finally the observer was removed and given the choice of either cocoa- or cinnamon-flavoured food. Each observer rat preferred the same flavour as their demonstrator had eaten and this preference was long lasting. Other studies have shown that rats can acquire a preference for up to four flavours simultaneously (Galef, Lee and Whiskin, 2005). This evidence suggests it is the interaction with other rats that have eaten a novel food that changes the preference for the food. Galef (1988) suggests this is due to an enhancement of the attractiveness of the novel food.

Imitation in predator avoidance

For many animals the first encounter with a predator may be the last. In other words avoiding predators is not something that can be learned by individual experience. A number of studies, including many that involved reintroducing species into the wild, have examined the role of social learning in learning how to react to a predator. For example, Griffin (2004) reviewed findings of social learning about predators in fish, birds and mammals. She suggests that some animals have evolved mechanisms to learn socially about danger. Such mechanisms are linked to classical conditioning. Fear responses are rapidly acquired in classical conditioning and require very few pairings of the UCS and the CS. Similarly, fear responses to predators are rapidly acquired from others.

A good example of this is the fear reactions that monkeys show when confronted with snakes. Wild monkeys have a strong fear reaction to snakes that includes fleeing, alarm calls and facial expressions. Monkeys that are raised in captivity do not show the same reaction, which suggests the fear of snakes is not innate (Pearce, 2008). Mineka and Cook (1988) have shown that if monkeys that have been raised in captivity observe the reaction of a wild monkey to a snake they will show the same responses. The response to the snake is shown even when the 'observer' monkey can no longer see the wild monkey's response and can last up to a year after the initial observation. Mineka and Cook (1988) suggest this is caused by a social variant of classical conditioning. They believe the fear shown by the wild monkey is the unconditioned stimulus that triggers fear (the unconditioned response) in the observer monkey. The snake then becomes the conditioned stimulus that triggers the conditioned response of fear.

Pearce (2008) calls this observational conditioning and points out that this process can play an important role in learning to avoid predators.

Vervet monkeys have a number of different calls for different predators such as eagles, leopards and snakes. The different calls produce different reactions that are appropriate for the type of predator they represent. When the vervet monkeys hear the eagle call they retreat from the tops of trees and look up. As eagles strike from above this is an appropriate behaviour. The response to the leopard call is to run to a tree and climb to the highest branches. Although leopards can climb, the very thin branches that will support monkeys will not support the weight of a leopard. The monkeys' response to the snake call is to stand on their hind legs and look at the ground (Seyfarth, Cheney and Marler, 1980). There is evidence that some aspects of the vervet calls are learned. Young vervets learn to discriminate between different objects during their first four years (Seyfarth and Cheney, 1986). For example, infants make eagle calls in response to many types of bird at first but as juveniles they only make the calls in response to birds of prey and then as adults they only make the calls when they see the eagles that prey on them. The young vervet monkeys also gradually learn to discriminate between mammals in general and leopards. This discrimination seemed to be learned from the imitation of the behaviour of other members of the troupe.

Summary

Social learning could be very useful to animals since it avoids the potentially lengthy process of learning by trial and error. There is some evidence that wild animals, such as rats, learn to select diet by copying others. Clearer evidence that the food preferences of rats can be influenced by others comes from experimental evidence. These show that rats prefer food sources that have been tried by other rats. However these findings may be explained by stimulus enhancement rather than imitation.

Another potential use of social learning is avoidance of predators. There is evidence that monkeys can learn fear reactions to predators by observing the reactions of others. This may be a form of classical conditioning called observational conditioning. Monkeys may also learn appropriate alarm calls for different types of predators from others.

Imitation could also be useful to learn to solve problems. There is some evidence of learning by imitation from naturalistic studies of birds and monkeys. However, this evidence is difficult to interpret. Clearer evidence of learning by imitation comes from experimental studies, which show, for example, that chimpanzees can learn to crack nuts by imitating others.

Machiavellian intelligence

Some animals live in complex social groups. Living in social groups can present problems that are not encountered by solitary animals. Those in social groups may need to learn to deal with others and to solve the problems that social relationships can bring (who to groom, who to share food with, who to dominate, who to submit to and so on). Humphrey (1976) suggested that the apparent superior intelligence in primates was not an adaptation to their environment but to the needs of complex social interaction. This was called the social intelligence hypothesis. This hypothesis was developed by Byrne and Whiten (1988a) into the Machiavellian intelligence hypothesis. The hypothesis is that **Machiavellian intelligence** is a particular type of social intelligence where animals learn not only to exist in a social group, but to deliberately manipulate others in the group. This could involve making and breaking alliances, misdirecting others or deceiving others in the social group for individual gain.

Byrne and Whiten (1988b) illustrate Machiavellian intelligence by describing a number of instances of baboons behaving in an apparently deceptive way to gain advantage. In one example, a juvenile baboon watched an adult dig up a large root. The juvenile then looked around and began to scream loudly. This attracted the attention of the juvenile's mother who was a dominant female in the troupe. She ran over and chased the other adult away. This left the juvenile free to pick up the abandoned root and eat it. Byrne and Whiten suggest the juvenile's scream was designed to mislead the mother and provoke an attack. However, this explanation raises the question of interpretation of intent of animal behaviour. Do the examples show deliberate attempts to deceive or are there other explanations? One alternative explanation is that the behaviour is a learned response that occurred because of past experience. If the juvenile had previously approached an adult who was eating and had been threatened, the normal response would be to scream. The scream would trigger an attack by the mother and the juvenile would be left with the food; it would be reinforced for screaming in the presence of a feeding adult. The apparent deception might be behaviour learned by operant conditioning.

In a second book on the topic, Whiten and Byrne (1997) reviewed the Machiavellian intelligence hypothesis in the light of the research and debate the first volume sparked. They note that evidence for the theory has emerged from a variety of observational and experimental studies. For example, Harcourt (1992) found that primates use alliances more than non-primates and choose their alliances on the basis of social 'value'. Harcourt and de Waal (1992) found that chimpanzees use alliances to gain influence from powerful individuals in the group. Both these examples suggest primates understand power relationships and use them. In a detailed analysis of relationships between three captive chimpanzees, de Waal (1986) found that one chimpanzee overturned a dominance relationship with an older male by challenging him in the presence of a third male. The support of the third male was crucial in the challenge and de Waal suggests this was the result of planning and social manipulation. There is evidence from a number of field playback experiments that primates and other monkeys recognize and respond differently to calls of different animals (for example Cheney and Seyfarth, 1999). The studies indicate knowledge of kinship and dominance relationships of other monkeys. There is also evidence of social, Machiavellian intelligence in a variety of animals other than monkeys. For example, Connor (2007) describes the alliance relationships found in a large group of bottlenose dolphins and claims that they are both complex and shifting. These complex alliances are mediated by a variety of behaviours that suggest a form of social intelligence. Holekamp, Sakai and Lundrigan (2007) suggest that spotted hyenas not only recognize their kin but third-party kin and rank relationships, and that they use this knowledge in social decision making.

One of the problems of the Machiavellian intelligence hypothesis is that it encompasses many different strands. For example, some researchers tend to refer to social intelligence as Machiavellian while others reserve the term for social manoeuvring and deception. For example, Strum, Forster and Hutchins (1997) have questioned what exactly is meant by Machiavellian intelligence. The general thrust is that social life is problematic and that an increase in intelligence is required to cope with these social problems. However Strum et al. suggest this leaves a number of unanswered questions such as, what is social complexity? A second question is exactly how does such social complexity affect individuals? Finally, they question what the link between social complexity and cognition really is. Barrett, Henzi and Rendall (2007) also question whether social complexity requires an increase in cognitive complexity. They suggest that social intelligence hypotheses tend to present an anthropocentric view of social life and cognition (that is, viewed from a human perspective). This leads to understanding social complexity in human terms and this may not be representative of the primate (or other species) social world.

Summary

Machiavellian intelligence is a particular type of social intelligence that enables animals to exist in a social group, and deliberately manipulate others in the group. This manipulation may involve shifting alliances, misdirection or deception for individual gain. There is evidence from observational studies of primates of behaviour to both manipulate alliances and deceive. More recent evidence has suggested that some non-primate species show similar signs of social intelligence particularly in manipulating alliances. However, most of the evidence is observational and this can be open to a number of interpretations. Questions have been raised about the exact nature of Machiavellian intelligence and why it should have developed.

Thinking scientifically →

Interpretation of observational evidence

Much of the evidence of intelligence in wild animals comes from observations of animals in their natural environment. Observations of animals in their natural environments reveal behaviour that might not be shown in captivity but they also demonstrate one of the problems of observational studies: interpretation of the evidence.

In observational studies of animals in a natural environment, there is a lack of control. The observers do not know how animals behaved before their study or what previous experiences might influence the behaviour of animals. The observers do not deliberately change variables to investigate the influence of any manipulation. These types of study cannot therefore establish cause and effect. There are often many ways of interpreting the data from the observational studies: however, in the absence of experimental data where one variable is deliberately manipulated while others are controlled, it is not possible to choose between them.

For example, the behaviour of the baboons described by Byrne and Whiten (1988b) could be explained in many ways. They did not manipulate the situation to investigate what effect it had and they did not know what had happened to the young baboon before their observation. It may be that baboons are capable of deliberately deceiving others but it is equally possible that the baboon had been reinforced for 'deception' in the past.

Theory of mind

Humans often explain behaviour by referring to a mental state (for example I ate because I was hungry). We also make inferences about the mental states based on their behaviour (for example he ate quickly therefore he must have been hungry). This ability to attribute mental states either to the self or to others is called **theory of mind** (ToM). These mental states might include intentions, beliefs, knowledge or lack of knowledge and emotions (Roberts, 1998). The question of whether animals may possess ToM was first raised by Premack and Woodruff (1978) after studying a chimpanzee named Sarah. They showed Sarah a number of videos of humans attempting to solve the problem of how to reach some bananas. Each of the videos stopped before the solution was shown. Sarah was given the choice of two photographs; one showed the person using a tool that would result in a successful solution and the other showed a behaviour that would not. She chose the one that would result in a successful solution in 21 of 24 trials. Does this suggest she inferred something about the mental state of the person in the video? In other words does it suggest that chimpanzees have a ToM? Pearce (2008) suggests there are two lines of evidence to investigate this: understanding the use of deception and knowledge attribution.

Understanding the use of deception

The concept of deception was discussed in relation to Machiavellian intelligence where the focus was on whether there was evidence that deception could be used for social advantage. It can also be used to investigate whether animals have a ToM. If an animal is aware that the behaviour of other animals is influenced by knowledge it might be capable of manipulating information to deceive others.

This was tested by Woodruff and Premack (1979) in an experiment with chimpanzees. Individual chimpanzees observed a person hide food under one of two containers before leaving the room. The chimpanzee could not reach the containers but could see them. In the next stage one of two trainers entered. The two trainers were dressed differently and behaved differently. One behaved in a 'cooperative' fashion and the other was a 'competitive' trainer. If the chimpanzee pointed to or stared at the correct container, the cooperative trainer gave it the food. However, the competitive trainer kept the food if the chimpanzee identified the correct container. Conversely, if the chimpanzee pointed to the wrong container with the cooperative trainer, it did not receive food, but with the competitive trainer it received the food. In order to get food in both conditions the chimpanzee had to deceive the competitive trainer.

Woodruff and Premack did find that some chimpanzees were able to get food in both conditions. Some chimpanzees seemed to mislead the competitive trainer and this could be evidence of a ToM. However, Pearce (2008) points out that there is more than one interpretation of these results. He notes that the study required many trials before there was evidence of 'deception'. During these trials the chimpanzee was reinforced for a different behaviour in the presence of a different trainer. The trainers are two different stimuli and the chimpanzee learns to discriminate between them because of operant conditioning. Given the wealth of evidence about the subtle behaviour changes that can be learned with operant conditioning, this seems to be a simpler, more parsimonious, explanation.

Knowledge attribution

If you see someone hide an object in a box you know that they know where the object is. This is because humans are able to attribute knowledge to others using a ToM. If animals can be shown to attribute knowledge to others this would be evidence of a ToM. There are a number of studies that have investigated this possibility. Povinelli, Nelson and Boysen (1990) used a 'guesser-knower' experiment with chimpanzees to investigate attribution. In the experiment four chimpanzees had to choose a correct cup in order to get food. The chimpanzees were tested individually in a room with two trainers. At the start of the study one of the trainers left the room. The trainer who remained placed food under one of four cups. The chimpanzee could see that food was being placed somewhere but the cups were hidden by a screen at this stage. The trainer who put the food in the cup was the 'knower' since they were the only person that knew which cup contained the food. The other trainer then returned and, since they did not witness where the food was placed, they were the 'guesser'. The screen was removed and the two trainers pointed to a different cup. The knower pointed to the correct cup and the guesser pointed to one of the incorrect ones. The trainers taking the roles of the knower and guesser varied on each trial, thus the chimpanzees could not simply learn a different behaviour in response to each trainer. If the chimpanzees can attribute knowledge to others they should infer that only the knower could identify the correct cup. They should have chosen the cup that the knower pointed to. Eventually all chimpanzees could do so and this may be taken as evidence for a ToM. However, it took many trials before they could do so reliably. In these trials the chimpanzee was rewarded with the food for choosing the knower but not for the guesser. It is possible they learned the association between the person who stayed and food (that is, the behaviour was due to operant conditioning not ToM). In a similar study with rhesus monkeys, Povinelli, Parks and Novak (1991) found that the monkeys did not learn to use the cue provided by the knower.

Povinelli and Eddy (1996) used a simple design to test chimpanzees' ability to attribute knowledge to humans. They first taught the chimpanzees to make a begging gesture in order to get food from trainers. During the test the chimpanzees were shown two trainers with the food between them. One of the trainers had a bucket over her head but the other did not. If the chimpanzees have a ToM they should make the begging gesture in front of the trainer with no bucket since they are the only one who can see. However, they failed to discriminate between the two and made the gestures to both trainers. This suggests they either do not have a ToM or they failed to understand the study. One possibility is that the study represented a completely unnatural situation for the chimpanzees.

In a completely different style of experiment, Tomasello, Call and Hare (2003) tried to use more natural behaviour to investigate ToM. The study involved a subordinate and a dominant chimpanzee, who were housed in different quarters separated by a test area. Both could see the test area through a window. In one condition both chimpanzees watched a trainer place some food behind a barrier. When they were both put into the test area the subordinate did not go to the food but left it to the dominant chimpanzee. In both the wild and in captivity subordinates do not interfere with a dominant chimpanzee's access to food. A similar procedure was followed in the second condition except this time the dominant chimpanzee could not watch as the food was hidden. In this condition the subordinate went straight to the food. Tomasello et al. (2003) suggest this is because the subordinate inferred that the dominant animal did not know that the food was hidden and it was therefore safe to go to it. If correct, this would be evidence for a ToM. However, Povinelli and Vonk (2003) question this interpretation. They suggest that the subordinate would have learned how to behave in the presence of the dominant chimpanzee through past experience. This experience would include being attacked if it approached food if the dominant chimpanzee was present. This learning extends to not approaching food if it was hidden when dominant visible. This shows social awareness but does not require a ToM.

Do non-human animals have ToM?

Call (2001) claims the evidence for ToM in animals remains elusive. He notes that on one side of the debate about ToM, researchers argue that animals, particularly chimpanzees, are capable of mental state attribution which indicates the presence of ToM. On the other hand, there are others who argue that all the evidence about ToM can be explained by learning about cues in the environment. For example, Heyes (1998) questions whether animals have theory of mind and believes all the findings of ToM research can be explained by conditioned discriminations. These do not require inferences about knowledge in another's mind. Call (2001) argues that neither of these positions is correct and that evidence from chimpanzees shows that they are doing more than just responding to cues but not necessarily showing an understanding of other animals' mental states. He suggests that the evidence shows that chimpanzees are able to extract knowledge from their experience and use this knowledge to solve social problems without needing a ToM. Penn and Povinelli (2007) have also commented on the lack of consensus about studies of ToM. They claim that the experiments used to test ToM are incapable of validating or falsifying the hypothesis that ToM exists in non-human animals and therefore have no value. Penn and Povinelli (2007) concluded that 'the problem is not that a ToM system has no value or is experimentally intractable; the problem is still no evidence that non-human animals possess anything remotely resembling one'. This conclusion is not shared by Tomasello and Call (2006) who assert that, while it is theoretically possible to explain all the knowledge attribution studies by behavioural rules, the 'rule' used to explain each experiment is different. Thus they argue that it is 'more plausible to hypothesize that apes really do know what others do' (Tomasello and Call, 2006, p. 371).

Summary

ToM is the ability to attribute mental states either to the self or to others. The question of whether non-human animals have ToM has been studied by investigating understanding deception and knowledge attribution. In a study of deception, chimpanzees had to learn a different behaviour with a competitive compared to a cooperative trainer in order to get food. Chimpanzees could do so and this may show ToM but the findings can also be explained by learning theory.

The ability to attribute knowledge to another would also show a ToM. In a guesser-knower study chimpanzees did learn to choose a cup indicated by the knower, suggesting they were capable of knowledge attribution. Clearer evidence seems to be shown by the different behaviour of a subordinate chimpanzee when a dominant one either had or had not seen food being hidden. However, the evidence for knowledge attribution in animals is not clear. Some researchers believe there is no study that indicates a ToM while others argue the evidence shows that some animals, particularly chimpanzees, know what others do.

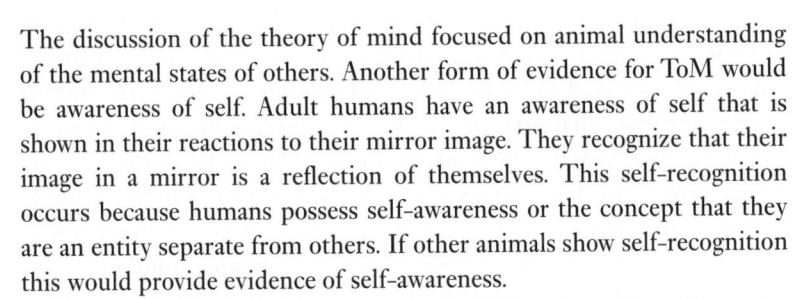

Self-recognition

The discussion of the theory of mind focused on animal understanding of the mental states of others. Another form of evidence for ToM would be awareness of self. Adult humans have an awareness of self that is shown in their reactions to their mirror image. They recognize that their image in a mirror is a reflection of themselves. This self-recognition occurs because humans possess self-awareness or the concept that they are an entity separate from others. If other animals show self-recognition this would provide evidence of self-awareness.

Observational studies of great apes with mirrors provide some evidence of self-recognition. Apes, like many other animals, initially seem to react to mirror images as other apes and show threat behaviour. However, unlike many other animals, the ape's behaviour changes and they soon show behaviour that indicates self-recognition. For example, Pearce (2008, p. 319) suggests that a mirror 'brings out the worst' in chimpanzees, such as using mirrors to pick their teeth, extract mucus from their nose or closely inspect their anal-genital area. These behaviours suggest that the chimpanzees are using the mirror image as a source of evidence about their bodies. Koko (a gorilla taught to use sign language) regularly uses a mirror for cleaning her teeth and grooming. There are a number of pictures on the Koko website and an interesting short video called 'Brilliant Pink' (see www.koko.org). In the video Koko is given a mirror to examine her tongue, which is coloured pink with ink. As she does so she also notices some glitter on her nose in the mirror and tries to wipe it off. This seems to suggest that she is capable of self-recognition.

However, this type of observational evidence is regarded by some as anecdotal. The objection to these studies is that it could be merely coincidental that the behaviours were observed while the animal was in front of a mirror (Pearce, 2008). The contention is the animals might have shown the same behaviour if the mirror was absent. This contention has been tested using experimental studies. One study by Povinelli et al. (1997) used chimpanzees that were already familiar with mirrors. They applied a dye to one eyebrow and the top of the opposite ear of each animal. They then recorded how often the animals touched these areas and two unmarked control areas in a 30-minute baseline period with no mirror. In the next 30-minute period they allowed the chimpanzees to look in mirrors and again recorded how often they touched both the marked and the unmarked areas. During the baseline there was very little touching of the dyed areas or the control areas. However, when looking in a mirror there was a large increase in the frequency that the chimpanzees touched the marked areas but they did not touch unmarked control regions any more than baseline levels. This result is difficult to dismiss as coincidence and the experiment provides better evidence for self-recognition. A further study by Povinelli, Rulf, Landau and Bierschwale (2003) suggested that self-recognition does not emerge in chimpanzees until they are over four years old and declines in later adulthood. The appearance of self-recognition in young animals seems consistent with a notion of emerging awareness. However, the finding that it declines in later adulthood is difficult to explain.

The evidence for self-recognition seems largely confined to the great apes (Anderson and Gallup, 1997). Most other animals, including Old

World and New World monkeys, cats, dogs and parrots, treat their mirror image as another animal not as a reflection of themselves. There are some exceptions, notably dolphins and elephants. Although it is difficult to replicate the chimpanzee studies with dolphins because they cannot touch marked areas of their bodies, there is some evidence of self-recognition. For example, after marking parts of a dolphin's body Reiss and Marino (2001) found they examined these parts in mirrors more than parts that had been touched but not marked. Further studies have shown that elephants can use mirrors to touch marked areas with their trunk (Plotnik, de Waal and Reiss, 2006). Plotnik et al. argued that elephants, like chimpanzees, live in socially complex groups. They tested three Asian elephants using a large mirror in the elephants exercise yard. All the elephants seemed to use the mirror to inspect themselves but only one of the three showed evidence of inspecting a paint mark on the forehead. However, this is consistent with studies of apes which show that only some respond to marks seen in a mirror.

The studies of the great apes, dolphins and elephants show that some animals can use mirrors to guide responses to their bodies. Some regard this as evidence for self-recognition but this interpretation is not universally accepted. For example, Heyes (1998) argues such evidence does not warrant ascribing the concept of self-recognition or self-awareness and offers an alternative explanation that is based on the idea of body concept. The argument is that a body concept would allow an animal to discriminate between stimuli from its body and stimuli from outside. If an animal learned to correlate mirror information with stimuli from its body, it could react appropriately to the mirror image. This does not require an awareness of self to explain the findings.

Some recent findings have shown that self-recognition may not be confined to social mammals with large brains. Prior, Schwarz and Güntürkün (2008) conducted a mark test with five magpies. They marked all the birds with either coloured paint or black paint in different conditions. The black paint acted as a control condition since it was difficult to see on the black feathers of the birds. Prior et al. found that two of the magpies showed clear evidence of recognizing the coloured paint and one showed weaker evidence. None of the birds reacted to the black paint. The finding that only some of the birds showed self-directed behaviour is consistent with findings from both chimpanzees and elephants. Prior et al. believe they have found evidence of self-recognition in an animal without a **neocortex**. Previous researchers had suggested that it was the neocortex, a relatively recent brain structure in evolutionary terms, which enabled large-brained mammals to recognize themselves. Toda and Watanabe (2008) used a different experimental procedure to test whether pigeons could recognize themselves. They assessed the pigeons' ability to distinguish between live video images of themselves and video images that had been pre-recorded. They found that the pigeons learned to peck more when shown the live images. They then introduced delay periods of 1, 3, 5 and 7 seconds to the live images. The pigeon's response rate increased as the time delay decreased. Toda and Watanabe suggest this is comparable to three-year-old human children who are unable to identify themselves if a two-second delay is introduced to a video image. It is also further evidence that self-recognition is not confined to social mammals.

Summary

Self-recognition in humans reflects our awareness of ourselves. If animals show self-recognition this may indicate some degree of self-awareness. This has been investigated by studying animals' responses to mirrors. After initially treating a mirror image of themselves as another animal, some, notably the great apes, seem to use the image in a way that indicates self-recognition. The apes use mirror images to inspect their bodies and to groom themselves.

However, this observational evidence has been dismissed by some, as the behaviour in front of the mirror could be coincidental. A number of experimental studies have been used to compare how often animals touch areas of their body that have been marked compared to areas that have not. These studies show a marked increase in the touching of marked areas compared to baseline levels but no increase in the touching of non-marked areas. Such findings have been replicated in most great ape species and with dolphins and elephants. However, the interpretation that this represents self-recognition or self-awareness is not shared universally. There is evidence that self-recognition is not confined to social mammals with large brains and that it is shown by some species of birds.

Metacognition

Metacognition is knowledge about one's own cognitive processes (Matlin, 2009). It has been variously described as 'thinking about thinking' or 'knowing about knowing'. Metacognition is recognized as being a very important part of human intelligence (for example Sternberg, 1983). This may be because the ability to reflect on memory and knowledge contribute to the ability to learn. Metacognition seems very limited in young children but increases during childhood (Flavell, 1979). This increase is probably responsible for improvement in memory seen during childhood (Matlin, 2009).

Recently there has been discussion among comparative psychologists about whether animals are capable of metacognition. Smith (2009) points out that metacognition is a sophisticated human capacity and that it rivals language 'in its potential to establish important continuities and discontinuities between human and animal minds' (p. 389). He also notes that traditional methods of studying human metacognition, which involve introspection and verbal responses, are not suitable for exploring animal metacognition. Animal studies of metacognition require researchers to infer metacognition from responses to behavioural tasks. For example, Call (2006) has reviewed a variety of tasks to test for reasoning and metacognition in animals. In one study dolphins and humans were given a discrimination task in which they had to decide whether a tone was high or low in pitch. They then had to press the HIGH key or the LOW key to indicate which type of tone they had heard. Some tones were clearly in the high or low category but others were on the border between the two. Correct responses were rewarded and incorrect responses were followed by a time-out period. The participants also had the opportunity of using a third key, the escape key. If participants pressed this key the session skipped to the next trial. The question being addressed was: would participants use the escape key in the hard-to-discriminate trials? If they did, they would show they knew what they did not know, or metacognition. Both the humans and dolphins did use the escape key more often in the difficult discrimination trials. Call (2006) concludes this shows dolphins know when they are uncertain. However, this conclusion is challenged by Shettleworth and Sutton (2006). They believe the use of the escape key can be explained by associative learning. The use of the escape key with some tones avoids the time-out periods and maximizes the reinforcements the animal receives. Thus the use of the escape key could be due to operant conditioning rather than metacognition.

Call (2006) also discusses the use a different paradigm to investigate metacognition. This examined whether animals would seek additional information when making a choice with incomplete information. In this study two-year-old children, chimpanzees and orang-utans were presented with two opaque tubes, one of which contained food. In order to get this food reward, participants had to touch the correct tube. The food was placed in the tube in one of two conditions, visible and hidden. In the visible condition, participants saw which tube the food was put in. In the hidden condition, the participants knew one tube had food in it but could not see which one it was. The participants were allowed to look into one tube before making their choice. The question was whether they would do so more often in the hidden condition than the visible condition. The results showed that they did and this suggests both the children and the apes knew that they did not know where the food was and so sought further information. Furthermore when they looked into an empty tube both children and apes then chose the other tube. This suggests that when the food was not in the empty tube they knew it was in the other. Call (2006) claims apes (and children) know what they have not seen, that they have metacognition. However, in a discussion about animal metacognition Shettleworth and Sutton (2006) claim that these and other findings can be explained by non-metacognitive strategies and that only rigorous controlled tests will reveal metacognitive abilities in animals.

Summary

Metacognition is knowledge about one's own cognitive processes and is important in the development of human intelligence. Metacognition is difficult to study in non-human animals because it requires the study of what they 'know' and this can only be inferred from behaviour. One such study sought to find out if animals know what they do not know by using a discrimination test. Correct answers in the test were rewarded and incorrect answers were followed by a time-out period. The animals were also given the option of an escape key which skipped to the next trial. The results showed the animals used the escape key on the hard-to-discriminate trials suggesting they knew when they did not know the correct response. However, the findings can also be explained by associative learning.

A different study investigated metacognition by studying whether animals sought more information before making choices with incomplete information. When animals saw food being placed in one of two tubes they did not look into them before choosing the correct one. Conversely, when they did not know which tube contained the food they sought further information by looking into one. This suggests they knew what they had not seen and did not know. However, some claim that all such findings can be explained by non-metacognitive strategies in animals.

Comparisons of intelligence in non-human animals

The discussion of evidence of non-human animal intelligence in this chapter has considered a number of species without really comparing species. However, it is clear that not all animals are the same in their ability to learn or process information. For example, we would not expect the same ability to process information in a chimpanzee and an earthworm. Does this mean some animals are more intelligent than others? People do regard different species as having varying levels of intelligence. For example, Nakajima, Arimitsu and Lattal (2002) asked students to rank a variety of animals in order of intelligence. Unsurprisingly chimpanzees were rated highest after humans followed by orang-utans and dolphins (earthworms were third from last above slugs and amoeba). However, is this common perception correct? Although it is clear there are differences in intelligence between vertebrates (such as chimpanzees) and invertebrates (such as earthworms) comparisons between vertebrates are challenging for a number of reasons.

Firstly, when making comparisons between animals one should not fall into the trap of thinking of some animals as 'primitive' and others 'advanced'. Dogs are not superior to snakes because mammals evolved from reptiles; both have evolved from a common ancestor several hundred million years ago. Similarly, humans have not evolved from chimpanzees; we have both evolved for millions of years from a common ancestor. Pearce (2008, p. 7) notes that 'it is no more possible to conclude that one species is more intelligent than another than it is to say that one is more evolved than the other. All that can be said is that the species have developed different intellectual abilities that enable them to survive in their particular environments.'

Roberts (1998) notes two other factors to consider when trying to compare degrees of intelligence in different animals. One is that simple comparisons tend to be quantitative (that is, are dogs more intelligent than cats?). However, research suggests that differences between animals may be qualitative rather than quantitative. In other words animals may differ in *what* they can learn rather than the *amount* they can learn (for example Bitterman, 1975). The other consideration is the natural environment of the animal. Roberts calls this the ecological approach and notes that this suggests behaviours or cognitive processes evolve to meet the environmental demands on a species. He illustrates this approach with a study on four species of corvids (crow family) by Olson, Kamil, Balda and Nims (1995). They found that some North American corvids had a better spatial memory than others because they needed to store more food for winter. However, tests of other forms of memory showed no difference.

These factors, and a large body of experimental evidence, have led to the null hypothesis of intelligence (Macphail, 1985). This suggests that there is no difference in the intelligence level of all vertebrates (with the exception of humans, for reasons discussed in later chapters). Pearce (2008) suggests that there is much evidence to support this hypothesis when considering associative learning (discussed in Chapter 2) but that the evidence is less convincing when considering learning that requires information processing (discussed in this chapter).

Further reading

Emery, N., Clayton, N. and Frith, C. (2008) *Social Intelligence: From Brain to Culture*. Oxford: Oxford University Press.

Hurley, S., and Nudds, M. (eds) (2006) *Rational Animals*. Oxford: Oxford University Press.

Pearce, J.M. (2008) *Animal Learning and Cognition: An Introduction* (3rd edn). Hove: Psychology Press.

Chapter 4

Language in non-human animals

Using human language is a very complex skill and many would regard it as our most important intellectual ability (Lund, 2003). In the chapters on human intelligence, it will become clear that language forms an important part both of our view of what intelligence is and in intelligence testing. In any examination of animal intelligence it is therefore useful to consider whether animals have the ability to use language. For a number of decades, there has been an argument between those who are convinced that animals can use language to a degree and those who believe that animals show no signs of using language. Lewin (1991) characterizes the two positions as the continuity school and the discontinuity school. The continuity school views the human ability to use language as an advanced version of some of the abilities shown by non-human animals. This school of thought claims that, although no non-human animal has the same level of ability to use language as humans, some animals demonstrate most of the major features of a language. Non-human animals just demonstrate these abilities to a lesser degree than humans do. These researchers suggest therefore that there is a quantitative difference between human and non-human animals. The discontinuity school on the other hand views the ability to use language as uniquely human and one that sets us apart from other animals. This view is that animal communication is qualitatively different to human language. This debate and implications for understanding animal intelligence form the basis of this chapter.

This chapter will cover:
- What is language in non-human animals?
- Does language exist in the wild?

- Teaching language to non-human animals
- Criticisms of animal 'language' learning studies
- Is language exclusive to humans?

What is language in non-human animals?

There are a number of reasons why the debate about animal language abilities divides researchers, but one of the main factors is the sophistication of human language. The use of language is one of the most complex human skills and it is difficult to agree an exact definition. Harley (2001), for example, claims many psychologists believe that, given the complexity of language, a formal definition is pointless. Yet without a clear definition of language it is very difficult to assess whether animals can use it or not. He suggests that language can only be described in terms of its many features such as semantics, syntax and pragmatics. Similarly, Hockett (1960) outlined 16 design features that can be used to describe human language. Some of these are not appropriate for animals because they refer to spoken language. However, there are a number of these features of language that are useful criteria to assess evidence of whether animals can use language. Brown (1973) regards **productivity, displacement** and **semanticity** as the three most important characteristics of language. These characteristics are significant because they seem to distinguish human language from simple animal communication.

Productivity refers to the ability of human language to combine and recombine words to produce an almost infinite variety of sentences. All human languages have a system of grammar (syntax) that enables us to produce and understand sentences, even if the sentence is completely novel. Thus humans are able to produce and understand messages they have never heard before. On the other hand, animal communication is not productive. Animal communication is restricted to very few signals that are used to produce a fixed message, such as an alarm call. These signals are reflexive or stimulus-bound; in other words communication is used to send signals about what is physically present. For example, alarm calls are produced if, and only if, a predator is detected. On the other hand, using language humans can discuss things that are not present in time or space. This ability – displacement – allows us to talk about the past and future or about objects that are not visible. For example, we can talk about some danger we faced yesterday or about the threats posed by polar bears, even if the nearest one is many miles away. Language is not stimulus-bound: it is voluntary and could be described as 'intentional communication'. The third feature mentioned by Brown (1973) is semanticity. This is the use of symbols, or words, to represent objects or concepts. The words therefore have meaning and this allows humans to communicate about objects and also about ideas and thoughts.

In addition to these three characteristics there are a number of other features of human language that are very different from animal communication. One of those features is **prevarication**, which is the ability to use language to deliberately deceive others (to lie). We can also use language to talk about absurdities or the impossible. So for example, you could tell somebody that there was a sabre-toothed tiger behind them but this would be both a lie, impossible and absurd. In contrast, most animal communication is in response to a stimulus and it therefore seems to be incapable of prevarication. Although the ability to use language is universal there are thousands of different human languages (that is, the language we use is not species specific). This is because of **traditional transmission**; we learn a particular language from the previous generation.

These features of language are very important for human intelligence. For example, productivity allows humans to talk about new information and concepts. Many human artefacts that are common now (computers, DVDs, mobile phones and so on) did not exist a few years ago yet we are able to discuss them. Displacement allows that discussion even if the object is not here. This means we are able to communicate about abstract concepts. Semanticity means that our words and communication have meaning to others. When someone talks about a mobile phone you understand what it is and can form a mental image of one. Prevarication allows us to use language to deceive but it also allows us to talk about the impossible; we can make up stories. Traditional transmission is one of the foundations of human culture. As human populations spread they gradually developed a variety of languages, which, in part, helps define cultural groups.

Aside from the problem of complexity of language, the question of whether non-human animals can use language faces other difficulties. As with most questions about animal cognition and intelligence, there is a problem of methodology and interpretation. Animals cannot use language in exactly the same way as humans because they do not have the appropriate vocal apparatus. Savage-Rumbaugh and Brakke (1996) point out that because animals cannot speak they must be taught an alternative system of producing language (such as signing or the use of symbols). However, this introduces methodological problems that make comparisons between species difficult. They believe this difficulty can potentially shift the focus away from the 'functional aspects of symbolic representation' to the mechanisms of the communication (that is, the emphasis of discussion shifts to how communication takes place rather than on what is communicated). Shettleworth (1998) points out that no non-human animal species can show exactly the same abilities as an adult human even if they could talk since they have evolved differently. Shettleworth suggests that the question we should ask about animals and language is what aspects, if any, of human language can be acquired by another species? She suggests that the key characteristic to investigate is productivity. That is, the focus should be to find whether there is any evidence that animals can learn grammatical rules in order to combine signals to produce new meanings.

Thinking scientifically →

Definitions of complex concepts

Harley (2001) suggests many psychologists believe that a formal definition is pointless because of its complexity. This causes a problem: how can we study what we cannot define? If language is too complex for simple definitions, how can we compare evidence of possible animal language? It is possible that one researcher's definition of what an animal language may be is very different to another's definition. All research has to start with some operational definitions of the concept or construct being studied but the research in this area is hampered by a lack of agreement about a definition. The debate about whether animals are capable of understanding and producing 'language' hinges on the definition of what such a language could be.

Some researchers believe that the complexity of language can be used to dismiss evidence that animals may be capable of a limited version of language. For example, Shanker, Savage-Rumbaugh and Taylor (1999) claim that 'ape language research has been marked by constantly shifting demands made by those who feel that only human beings can acquire language'. In other words, those from the discontinuity school can always find some aspect of language that is only produced by humans. On the other hand, those from the continuity school can point to language-like features of animal communication and claim it is evidence of a primitive 'language' or protolanguage. Without a clear definition of language, the debate is likely to continue.

Does language exist in the wild?

Nearly all animals communicate to others of the same species in some way. Even the simplest of animals, such as amoebae, can communicate in some way (Bonner, 1969). Animal communication typically does not show productivity, semanticity, displacement or prevarication. However, some communication systems do show some of these features and it is worth considering whether these are evidence of language in the wild. This section cannot consider the communication of all animals but will briefly review communication in some cetaceans (aquatic mammals) and primates. It starts with a surprising candidate for a natural non-human animal language, the honeybee (an insect with a very small brain compared to cetaceans and primates).

Honeybees

Honeybees have a system of communication that is used to indicate the location of a food source. If one bee finds a food source others soon follow. The mechanism by which bees recruit fellow workers was shown in a series of studies by von Frisch (1950, 1974). He discovered a complex form of communication that uses two types of dance to transmit information. The type of dance used depends on the distance of the food source. If the food source is near (within approximately 50 metres) the bee performs a round dance. This consists of turning left and right alternately in more or less the same spot and for about 30 seconds. This stimulates other bees to find the nearby food source by foraging.

When the food source is further away bees perform a more intricate dance called the waggle dance. The waggle dance involves the performance of a figure of eight movement by moving in a straight line, circling to the left to the start of the line and then following the line again before turning right. It is called the waggle dance because as a bee travels along the straight line it waggles its abdomen. Von Frisch (1974) found that this dance gave indications of both the direction and distance of a food source. He discovered this by placing food sources (sugar) at various locations around a hive. When a bee first found a particular source, he marked it with paint and then went to the hive to observe its behaviour. He found that the distance of the food source from the hive was indicated by the length of the straight part of the dance or the number of waggles of the abdomen (since a longer straight line allowed more waggles it is not clear which was the signal). The direction of the food source was indicated by the angle of the straight line relative to vertical. This angle represented the angle of the food source relative to the direction of the sun from the hive. If the food source was 45 degrees to the right of a line between the hive and the sun, the straight line was 45 degrees to the right of vertical.

The waggle dance shows some of the characteristics of language such as displacement (the dance indicates something that is not present) and interchangeability (bees can both perform and respond to the dance). However, there are many important features of language which are not shown in the bee dance. The key problem is that the dances show no evidence of productivity. Bees do not use the dance to produce different messages apart from distance or direction. It is a purely functional system for maximizing food gathering.

Cetaceans

Many researchers believe a more fruitful source of a natural non-human animal language might be among the cetaceans. Like humans, the cetaceans have large brains, they use complex auditory signals to communicate and many species are social. Some species of whale produce elaborate sequences of sounds that have been termed 'songs'. For example, the humpback whale produces a song that is highly structured. The songs have basic elements called units. These are combined into phrases which are then joined together to make a theme. Recordings of songs suggest they can consist of up to ten themes. Humpback whales from different areas show differences in their songs. The songs seem to have a social function. If a song is broadcast from a ship's underwater speakers, humpback whales in the area stop singing and swim towards the source of the new song (Tyack, 1983).

Dolphins are noted for their intelligent behaviour in captivity. There are many species of dolphin and most are very vocal and use a wide variety of sounds both in captivity and in their natural environment. These sounds are grouped into two types, pulsed and unpulsed. The pulsed types are high frequency sounds that include clicks and some ultrasound (that is, beyond human hearing range). The unpulsed sounds tend to be whistles and squeaks. It is possible that these sounds have a social function as schools of dolphins are very vocal (Herman, 2002). There is some evidence that different sequences of clicks may act as a way of identifying group members.

Although it is possible to record the sounds produced by cetaceans in their natural environment, it is very difficult to understand the function of these sounds. The environment in which they are produced, the open sea, makes it difficult for human investigators to know what the sounds are used for. The human investigators rarely know which animal has produced the sound or what effect it has, if any, on any recipients. Pearce (2008) points out that because little is known about the sounds produced by dolphins, it is conceivable that they may be a system of communication that approximates language. However, he argues that language enables humans to interact in very complex ways and that there is little naturalistic evidence of this type of complex interaction among dolphins.

Primates

Monkeys and apes have relatively large brains and are able to learn readily. Some species of primates, such as monkeys and apes, communicate by using a wide range of sounds and gestures. It is possible that some species may use a communication system that is similar to language. As mentioned in the previous chapter, one type of monkey that seems to have a complicated system of communication about predators is the vervet monkey. They have a number of different calls for different predators (eagles, leopards and snakes) which produce different reactions that are appropriate for the type of predator they represent. For example, if they hear the alarm call for an eagle the vervet monkeys retreat from the tops of trees to the centre and look up. As eagles strike from above, this is the best way to avoid them. The response to a leopard alarm call is the opposite. The monkeys run to trees and climb to the top since leopards are not supported by the thin branches that will support monkeys. On hearing the snake call, the monkeys stand on their hind legs to gain height and look around at the ground. These same responses are triggered if the calls are made via a loudspeaker (Seyfarth, Cheney and Marler, 1980). This seems to be good evidence of a signal that shows semanticity, in other words each sound conveyed a different meaning.

There is evidence that the different calls made by the vervet monkeys are partly learned. Infant vervets do make different alarm calls but at first fail to discriminate (Seyfarth and Cheney, 1986). So, for example, they may make eagle alarm calls at the sight of many birds but as juveniles (during first four years) they gradually learn to make the call only when they see eagles. There is a similar process in gradually discriminating between mammals on the ground and leopards. This discrimination seems to be learned from the other members of the troupe and is therefore evidence of traditional transmission.

These studies of communication between monkeys in their natural habitat suggest that they demonstrate a number of the features of human language. The communication between the vervet monkeys seems to show both semanticity and traditional transmission. The section on Machiavellian intelligence in non-human species suggested that there is also evidence of the use of signals to deceive, or prevarication, in baboons. The problem with such studies is the lack of control (for example there is no record of the past behaviour) and therefore any conclusions rely on interpretation. There is also no evidence from studies of monkeys or apes in the natural environment that shows any evidence of the key feature of language: productivity. The signals they use to communicate are not combined to produce any new messages.

Summary

The study of non-human animal communication in the natural environment reveals some relatively complex systems that show some of the characteristics of human language. The honeybee dance shows displacement by communicating about the distance and direction of a food source that is not visible. Vervet monkeys use different alarm calls to represent different predators and show evidence of semanticity and traditional transmission. However, all animal communication in the natural environment shows a few features of human language only; none show the *full range* of features that distinguish language from communication. More importantly, no non-human system of communication shows any evidence of productivity or the use of grammar, which is needed for generating novel messages. Human language allows us to discuss new material, abstract concepts and possibilities. This does not happen in natural animal communication.

Teaching language to non-human animals

There is very little evidence that non-human animals have the ability to use anything like language in their natural environments. However, there is another way of examining the question of whether they are capable of using a language: to try to teach them how to use some form of language.

Early studies

There were a number of studies in the twentieth century that attempted to teach apes a spoken language. In one study a chimpanzee called Gua was raised in a home alongside a human child (Kellogg and Kellogg, 1933). Both Gua and the child were exposed to language but, although the child learned to speak language, the chimpanzee did not. However, there was some indication that Gua understood some spoken language. Hayes and Hayes (1951) also exposed a chimpanzee, Vicky, to language and in addition tried to train her to speak. Despite intensive training Vicky only learned to say four words. Both these attempts failed for the same reason: apes are incapable of producing the complex sequence of sounds that are needed for language. Humans have a specialized larynx and have fine control over the release of air from the lungs. We do not merely breathe when we speak; we release air in precise bursts to produce sentences. Apes cannot do this.

Teaching language through sign language

Apes may not be able to produce spoken language but they do have good control over their hands and fingers. Although their hands do not work in precisely the same way as humans, they are dexterous enough to produce sign language. Sign languages among humans, such as American Sign Language (ASL), are as complex and elaborate as any spoken language. If apes can use ASL then they would demonstrate that they have the intelligence needed to produce language.

The first to investigate the possibility that apes might be able to use a sign language were Gardner and Gardner (1969). They studied a young female chimpanzee called Washoe (named after the county in Nevada where the study took place). Unlike previous studies, the Gardners did not speak to Washoe or to each other but instead created a 'signing environment' in which they, and the other humans who worked on the project, signed to each other and Washoe. Washoe was taught to make signs by moulding (putting her hands in the correct position) and operant conditioning (positive reinforcement for using signs). Sometimes she was reinforced with food but during the study it became evident that tickling also acted as reinforcement. Washoe did not learn many signs at first but then did slowly acquire the use of signs during the study. After about four years of training she could use about 160 signs clearly and consistently. The Gardners tested her ability to sign the name of objects using a double blind technique. This involved one trainer showing Washoe an object or picture while a second trainer, who could not see the first or the objects, recorded the signs that Washoe made. As well as nouns, Washoe was able to use verbs and pronouns. She could also combine signs in what seemed like an early form or grammar (for example 'Gimme drink' and 'Gimme tickle'). There was some evidence of longer combinations of signs such as when she signed 'Baby in my drink' after being shown a doll in her cup by a trainer. Washoe seemed able to produce novel combinations of signs. For example, when she was asked to name a swan she signed 'water bird'. Washoe seemed to be capable of displacement by signing about things that were not present. Some years after the initial study she adopted an infant called Loulis and would sign about him even if he was not in the room. Loulis was not taught ASL by humans but did learn some signs from Washoe, partly by imitation and partly because she moulded his hands to the correct position (Fouts, Hirsch and Fouts, 1982). This seems to be evidence of traditional transmission of the sign language.

A slightly different approach that used ASL was taken by Patterson (1978). Patterson studied a female gorilla called Koko and used both signs and spoken language in her presence. Like Washoe, Koko learned to use many signs and shows clear evidence of an ability to name objects. Unlike Washoe, she responded to both signs and spoken words and was able to respond to verbal questions with signed answers. Koko appeared to make up compound names for objects she did not know the sign for. For example, she referred to a cigarette lighter as a 'bottle match', a zebra as 'white tiger' and a Pinocchio doll as 'elephant baby' (Patterson, 1980). Over several decades Koko has learned the meaning of about 2000 words and can produce over a 1000 signs (Patterson and Matevia, 2001). She also can combine words in a non-random way which suggests the beginning of grammar (Patterson and Linden, 1981). During the course of the project Koko has been joined by other gorillas such as Michael. Koko showed clear signs of displacement by referring to Michael when he was not present. Koko appears to sign about emotional states. For example, when she seems to be angry she refers to herself as 'red mad gorilla'. Koko has had several pets and she achieved something of a celebrity status when one of her kittens (which she had named 'All Ball') died. Koko signed about, and appeared to show, her sadness about the death. However, any interpretation about what these signs refer to is difficult; we cannot understand what a gorilla 'feels'. Nevertheless the reference to

All Ball shows displacement. There is some evidence of prevarication in some of Koko's responses. For example, when asked about a window catch that she had clearly broken Koko blamed Kate (one of her trainers). Koko seems to have her own form of abuse for those who displease her; she calls them a 'big dirty toilet'!

Teaching language through symbols

Another group of researchers have used a different approach to teaching animals language by using symbols. There are a number of problems in using sign language. One is the problem of analysing the signs since an individual sign or combination of signs can be open to interpretation. Another problem is the difficulty of knowing whether a sign or combination is spontaneous, is in response to cues in the environment or imitation of the trainers. The use of symbols allows for more control and greater objectivity.

In one example of this approach, Premack (1971) used plastic shapes of various shape and colour to represent, or symbolize, words. The plastic shapes were used to study the use of language in a chimpanzee, Sarah. During the study Sarah learned to use approximately 130 shapes which were used to represent nouns, verbs, adjectives and so on. Premack was interested in whether Sarah could learn to use combinations of shapes to produce messages and she was required to put the shapes in the right order on a board. Sarah seemed able to do so and arranged the shapes in the right order to request things. She was also able to follow instructions that her trainer placed on the board. For example, if the sequence of shapes represented the message 'Sarah give me apple' she would do so (Premack, 1976). Premack tested Sarah's ability to answer questions about the relationships of objects. He found that if she was shown a red card on top of a blue card she could answer questions about the two cards correctly (that is, the question 'is the red card on top?' would be answered 'yes').

Rumbaugh (1977) used a different approach and used symbols on a keyboard (termed 'lexigrams') to represent words. The keyboard was connected to a computer, which allowed every response made by the animal to be recorded. Like Premack, Rumbaugh was interested in whether the apes could learn to use combinations of symbols in the right order to produce an artificial language. This language was called 'Yerkish' after the Yerkes Primate Research Center where the research took place. The first to be trained in the use of this new language was a chimpanzee called Lana. Lana learned to use the symbols in the right order to ask for things such as food. One interpretation of this is that she was able to learn about the order of the symbols. However, the responses can also be explained as learning a simple sequence of pushes to gain reinforcement (that is, by operant conditioning). For example, the sequence ‘please machine give grape’ requires pushing four symbols to gain a reward; it does not require any understanding of language. However, Lana’s responses showed she could recognize the difference between ‘Lana groom Tim’ and ‘Tim groom Lana’ which suggests some understanding of symbol order.

In subsequent studies Savage-Rumbaugh (1986) tried to investigate the learning of Yerkish by emphasizing the social use of the language with two chimpanzees, Sherman and Austin. The chimpanzees were successfully trained to use the lexigram to request tools to open food containers and to request food from each other. There were also tests to determine whether they could show displacement. In one study they were shown a display of food and drink in one room. They were then taken to another room and asked to use the lexigram to choose an item from the display (which was now out of view). When they returned to the room with the display they could eat or drink the item if they picked the one they had chosen on the lexigram. They were able to do this with 90 per cent accuracy (Rumbaugh and Savage-Rumbaugh, 1994). This seems to be good evidence of displacement.

Teaching language through early exposure

One of the most interesting studies of language learning by a primate happened by accident. Rumbaugh and Savage-Rumbaugh (1994) decided to try to teach Yerkish to bonobos (pygmy chimpanzees) using a lexigram. Bonobos are vocal and highly social and the researchers believed they might learn better than the common chimpanzee. The first study was of an adult female bonobo, Matata, but she failed to learn to use the lexigram well. However, during the study Matata was accompanied by a young male bonobo, Kanzi, who she had adopted. Although Rumbaugh and Savage-Rumbaugh did not try to teach Yerkish to Kanzi, he started to use the lexigram to name and ask for things. He also showed signs of understanding spoken English. It seemed as if Kanzi was learning some Yerkish and English simply by being exposed to them at an early age (Kanzi was six months old when the study began).

The realization that Kanzi seemed to be learning more from exposure to a stimulating environment rather than formal training led to a change in the nature of the study. Kanzi was given a lot of human attention and was encouraged to roam in a large wooded area accompanied by humans who both spoke and communicated with him on a portable lexigram keyboard. After a number of years of this experience, controlled tests showed that Kanzi could both understand and produce messages on the lexigram and understand some spoken English. For example, he was able to follow simple instructions that used novel sentences such as 'Make the doggie bite the snake' and 'Get the apple from the fridge'. Precautions were taken to prevent any cueing by his trainers by giving instructions via headphones. If Kanzi was asked to collect an item from a particular location he was able to do so even if an identical item was in front of him. So if he were asked to get a carrot from the fridge he did so even if there was another carrot in full view. Savage-Rumbaugh et al. (1993) suggest that Kanzi had comprehension skills that were equivalent to that of a 2½-year-old child. However, his communication via the lexigram was only equivalent to the language production of a 1½-year-old child. Savage-Rumbaugh and Brakke (1996) suggest that Kanzi uses a simple version of grammar (a 'protogrammar'). They also believe that, although he does not use language in the same way as an adult human, he shows clear signs of language abilities. Kanzi seems to show the key features of semanticity, displacement and productivity. He shows understanding of the meaning of words and symbols, he can use them to refer to objects that are not present and can understand and produce new messages. Furthermore, he produces such messages with spontaneity rather than in response to prompts by trainers.

Savage-Rumbaugh and her colleagues have raised other young apes (including a bonobo, Panbanisha, and a chimpanzee, Panzee) in a similar fashion to Kanzi with similar success but have failed with older individuals. They have suggested that, like in humans, this may indicate that there is a sensitive period early in ape development when they need to be exposed to language.

Teaching language to dolphins

Much of the work on the ability to learn language in apes tried to assess both the comprehension and production of signs and sign combinations. In contrast, the study of dolphin language learning has concentrated mainly on comprehension. Herman and Morrel-Samuels (1996) suggest that it is difficult to obtain objective, replicable data from studies that emphasize productive skills. They believe that receptive skills are likely to be a better indicator of language potential since animals' behaviour following instructions can be objectively measured. Herman and his colleagues trained two bottlenosed dolphins to respond to sequences of signals (Herman, Richards and Wolz, 1984; Herman, Pack and Morrel-Samuels, 1993). One dolphin, Phoenix, was taught to respond to acoustic signals, which consisted of short computer generated noises. The other, Akeakamai, was taught to respond to hand and arm movements of a trainer by the pool. Both the acoustic signals and the gestures were used as a type of language with different signals to represent words. Some of these signals represented objects (ball, frisbee and so on), some represented actions (go, fetch) and some modifiers (in, on). The signals were combined in a particular form of grammar that was designed to test the dolphins' understanding of the word order and of novel combinations. The grammar of the combinations also ensured that the dolphins had to respond to the whole sequence rather than respond to each signal in turn. For example, the sequence 'basket ball in' means put the ball in the basket. The dolphins were tested on their ability to understand grammar by changing the order of signals. For example, a sequence 'surfboard swimmer fetch' means take the swimmer to the surfboard whereas 'swimmer surfboard fetch' means take the surfboard to the swimmer (Herman, 2006). The dolphins followed such instructions accurately and also learned to respond to novel four- and five-word signals that conveyed complex instructions. For example, Akeakamai correctly responded to 'hoop right frisbee fetch' (which, using the syntax Herman et al. created, means take the frisbee to the hoop on the right). Akeakamai also responded correctly to novel five-symbol combinations such as 'right basket left ball in' (which means put the ball on your left in the basket on the right) and 'left basket right ball in' (which means put the ball on your right in the basket on your left). The same five symbols in a different sequence led to different and appropriate behaviour.

Herman (2006) suggests these results show dolphins are able to understand two important components of language: semanticity (word meaning) and syntax (grammar). They showed understanding of a wide number of symbols that represented objects, actions and modifiers. They were also sensitive to word order, or grammar, and responded accurately to novel sentences. In further studies, Herman and his colleagues showed evidence of displacement. In one study Akeakamai was given two paddles to press in her pool. One paddle represented 'yes' and the other 'no'.

Akeakamai was then asked to report whether objects were present in her pool or not. She was able to correctly report when objects were not there. This shows spatial displacement since she was referring to an object that was not present. Akeakamai also showed temporal displacement by showing the correct response to an instruction about an object even when the object was placed in the pool after the instruction. Herman and his colleagues seem to provide strong evidence of understanding of grammar in dolphins and have shown that dolphins can respond appropriately to complex instructions. However, the approach they have adopted concentrates on language comprehension only. Pearce (2008) points out that language production is as important as language comprehension. Both are needed to truly show the ability to use language.

Summary

The various studies of apes using sign language, plastic shapes or lexigrams have shown that they are able to use symbols to communicate. Some of this communication shows some of the characteristics of language. All studies show that apes are able to use signs or symbols to name objects. This demonstrates semanticity. Some of the apes were able to show the appropriate responses to instructions given by signs or symbols (and in some cases spoken English). For instance, Kanzi can follow instructions given in English even when the instruction is a novel one. Many of the studies have shown that apes are capable of displacement and can use sign or symbols to refer to objects that are not present. There is also some evidence that some apes can demonstrate prevarication, although this evidence tends to be anecdotal. However, there is some question about the key characteristic of productivity. Although there is some evidence that primates are capable of understanding novel messages using a form of grammar, the evidence is not universally accepted. Research with dolphins has concentrated on the comprehension of symbols and grammar and has shown that dolphins are able to respond appropriately to different symbol order. However, the research with dolphins has focused on comprehension only.

Criticisms of animal 'language' learning studies

The excitement and enthusiasm generated by some of the early studies was tempered by the publication of 'Nim' by Terrace in 1979. Nim was a chimpanzee who was taught to use sign language. Terrace kept a detailed record of all the signs Nim made and the circumstances in which they were made. During the study he learned 125 signs and made them on 19,000 occasions. At first his use of signs seemed to be much like the development of language in a child. He began using one sign at a time but then gradually began to use two-sign sentences in combinations. However, unlike a human child, Nim failed to progress beyond this point. Terrace reports a number of reasons to suggest that Nim was not able to use the signs to produce language. Firstly, he did not use combinations of signs in a consistent manner (that is, he showed no concept of grammar). Secondly, Nim seemed to remain in the two-sign stage. Children gradually increase the length of sentence as they learn more words and grammar. Any increase in Nim's signing was caused by repetition (for example banana Nim banana Nim). Finally, analysis of the context of signing showed a tendency for Nim to imitate or repeat the signs of his trainers rather than using them spontaneously. Terrace concluded that Nim was able to imitate signs and to use simple sequences to gain food reward but that he showed no evidence of learning a language.

Terrace, Petitto, Sanders and Bever (1979) reviewed evidence both from the Nim study and studies of other apes using signs to ask: 'Can an ape create a sentence?' Using detailed analysis of both the signs made by the apes and the context in which a sign was made, they concluded the answer was 'no' for a number of reasons. When children learn a language they show a progression from single words to two words and then to longer utterances that have a consistent grammar. All the apes they reviewed did not do this. For example, Nim produced an average length of signing of 1.5. One of his longest 'sentences' was 'give orange me give eat orange me eat orange give me eat orange give me you'. This shows a lack of grammar, and repetition. In other words, Nim and others fail to show Shettleworth's (1998) key feature of language, productivity. Another feature of a child's use of language is spontaneity; they produce language without being prompted. In contrast, the apes reviewed by Terrace et al. rarely did so but tended to respond to prompts by trainers. Terrace et al. also found that sequences of signs that might pass for 'sentences' were actually the result of imitation of trainers or were in response to cues. For example, careful analysis of the famous sequence of Washoe signing 'Baby in my drink' suggests this apparently spontaneous sequence was in response to cues from the trainer.

These conclusions were shared in a later study by Rivas (2005). The study reviewed evidence from five chimpanzees, including Washoe, and found no evidence that they use any form of grammar. Rivas also noted that 86 per cent of the signs and combinations of signs were requests for something the chimpanzee wanted. This leads to the criticism that ape language studies merely show the effect of operant conditioning. In other words, the animals produce the signs because they have been conditioned to do so for food not because they 'understand' them. It is a simple procedure to teach a pigeon to peck a sequence of disks to get food but this is not regarded as language. This raises the question of whether learning a sequence of signs to gain food is any different. It prompts the question 'does the use of a sign language promote the illusion of language?' However, Shettleworth thinks it is a mistake to dismiss the evidence from these studies as mere conditioning. She points out that:

> Much of the controversy in this area boils down to disagreement over whether the subjects 'really' have one or another of linguistic competence – syntax, reference, etc – or whether their behaviour is 'merely' instrumental responding. **(Shettleworth, 1998, p. 562)**

She thinks it is paradoxical that we recognize that conditioning can produce elaborate representations of the world but if communication is interpreted as the result of conditioning it is seen as simple.

Most of the questions raised by Terrace et al. (1979) and Rivas (2005) about the ability of apes to use sign language are based on studies of common chimpanzees. They do not appear to take into account evidence about Kanzi and other bonobos studied by Savage-Rumbaugh and her colleagues. Kanzi has learned language in a different way than the chimpanzees and seems to show semanticity, displacement and productivity (Savage-Rumbaugh et al., 1993). He also seems to use language spontaneously rather than merely in response to trainers. Since Kanzi learned much of his use of symbols by observation rather than training and reward, it is harder to dismiss this as merely evidence of operant conditioning.

Summary

Following the study of Nim and a review of other apes using sign language, Terrace and his colleagues concluded that apes do not show evidence of language learning. They claim that the apes do not show any evidence of consistent sign order, or grammar. The apes do not use signs spontaneously but in response to trainers. Many of the sequences of signs in apes seem to be the result of imitation of trainers or responses to cues. There is also a suggestion that signs and sequences of signs were produced for reinforcement. The signs were produced by behaviour shaping but give the illusion of being a language.

Is language exclusive to humans?

At the beginning of the chapter it was noted that there is a disagreement between the continuity school and the discontinuity school views about animal language. Lewin (1991) suggests there is a divide between those who believe that there is a quantitative difference in human language and animal language and those who believe that the difference is qualitative. There is a large range of studies of the great apes and other species such as bottlenosed dolphins but much of this evidence continues to cause disagreement. Despite analysing the same evidence there is still disagreement between the two schools.

Chomsky (1972) is from the discontinuity school and believes that there is a qualitative difference between human language and animal communication. He believes that language is unique to humans. He suggests that only humans have an innate mechanism called the language acquisition device (LAD). The LAD allows all humans to acquire language merely by being exposed to it. Although all languages are superficially different, they all have certain features, or universals, that can be recognized by the LAD. Since animals do not have an LAD they cannot learn language like humans but merely imitate it. A similar view is taken by Vauclair (1990). He suggests that most complex cognitive activities show continuity between animals and humans but that language does not. He suggests that human language is the result of a unique combination of biological and social evolution (see Chapter 5). This he believes has resulted in an ability that is qualitatively different from that of animals.

In contrast Savage-Rumbaugh and her colleagues argue that animals do have the ability to use some form of language. Greenfield and Savage-Rumbaugh (1990) agree that there is a genetic basis to human language but point out that it is likely to be affected by a large number of genes. Since we share so many of our genes with apes (particularly chimpanzees), it is probable that chimpanzees and other apes will share some of this genetic basis for language. They have reviewed the evidence about language comprehension and production in bonobos and believe the question is not 'Can animals learn language?' but 'What level of language development are animals capable of achieving?' The question is of quantity not quality. Greenfield and Savage-Rumbaugh (1990) also suggest there is a double standard in interpreting the language of young children and the use of symbols or signs in apes. In children any combination of words or novel use of words is seen as evidence of a stage of language development since they ultimately develop adult human language. However, apes do not go on to develop the equivalent of an adult human language. Therefore any novel use of words or any evidence of simple forms of grammar is not regarded as being evidence of language.

Pearce (2008) highlights a different problem with the research into non-human animal language, particularly with apes. He suggests that the failure to produce any evidence of language abilities may be caused by a lack of motivation rather than a lack of intelligence. The animals may simply not want to communicate beyond the need to get food rather than be unable to use signs or symbols. It may be no coincidence that those apes that had the most formal training and uninteresting environment (such as Nim) failed to show evidence of spontaneous or productive language. On the other hand, apes who had more stimulating environments, such as Kanzi, showed the most spontaneous and productive language. Shettleworth (1998) points out that Kanzi only developed his linguistic skills after intensive exposure to language and a lot of attention from adult humans. This might be exceptional for an ape but such an experience is the norm for children. Savage-Rumbaugh, Rumbaugh and Fields (2006) suggest that, like children, apes may learn from stimulating environments and close ties with caregivers. Those apes that have such backgrounds show the highest level of linguistic ability. In contrast training without stimulation or close ties is simply rote learning divorced from communication.

Another problem in answering the question of whether language is unique to humans is that the concept of language is not clearly defined. This produces difficulties for researchers trying to find evidence of language in non-human species. Shanker et al. (1999) claim 'ape language research has been marked by constantly shifting demands made by those who feel that only human beings can acquire language'. Psychologists constantly pose new demands of evidence for those trying to demonstrate that it is possible to teach animals language. Shanker et al. (1999) suggest that it would be more productive to explore what the apes can do rather than search for evidence of language skills that the apes do not have.

Finally, there may be reasons, other than purely scientific ones, why the debate about animal language is so fiercely argued. As Shettleworth (1998, p. 562) notes:

> Given how closely the results of language-training projects bear on ideas about what makes us human, controversy about them is likely to continue.

If it can be shown that animals can master language to a degree then the view that some people have of being separate from, and superior to, animals is challenged.

Summary

The debate about whether non-human animals are capable of learning language is interesting and complex. Despite the wealth of evidence accumulated from over four decades of research, there is still little agreement about whether animals can learn language. The discontinuity view is that there is a qualitative difference between animal communication and human language. This qualitative difference means that no matter what training or experience an animal has its communication will never show the true characteristics of human language. The continuity view on the other hand suggests that there is evidence that animals, particularly apes, can learn some language skills. This view is that there is merely a difference in the amount the animals can learn. One factor that needs to be taken into account is the level of stimulation animals receive. Children are exposed to rich environments with close adult attention and not all apes have had a similar early experience. Finally, until psychologists can agree on precisely what they mean by 'language' this debate is likely to continue.

Further reading

Anyone who wishes to explore the debate about animal language in more detail should compare the views expressed in the following two books:

Wallman, J. (1992) *Aping Language.* Cambridge: Cambridge University Press.

Savage-Rumbaugh, E.S. and Lewin, R. (1994) *Kanzi: The Ape at the Brink of the Human Mind*. New York: John Wiley & Sons.

These two books represent very different viewpoints and clearly set out the discontinuity and continuity positions.

See also:

Terrace, H.S., Petitto, L.A., Sanders, R.J. and Bever, T.G. (1979) Can an ape create a sentence? *Science,* 206, 891–900.

Much of the evidence about ape 'language' and other abilities above is difficult to describe fully. A more detailed picture emerges from watching video footage of some of the 'stars' of this research, Washoe, Koko and Kanzi. Use these as key words to find information and video footage of the apes. In particular look for:

Friends of Washoe
Koko foundation
Great Ape Trust (includes Kanzi and other bonobos and chimpanzees)

Chapter 5

Evolution of human intelligence

As I write this on a computer, it is –3°C outside yet I am warm inside a centrally heated house. In the background, I can hear music playing on a digital radio. All this is possible because of human ingenuity. Humans are intelligent animals and the evidence of this intelligence surrounds us. Our environment no longer shapes us; we shape our environment for our comfort and entertainment. Humans (*Homo sapiens*) are, in evolutionary terms, a very new species that first appeared between 200,000 and 150,000 years ago. Yet in this short time we have been able to dominate the planet. Humans now occupy every continent on the planet and are able to survive in the hottest and coldest environments on Earth because of culture and technology. All humans are capable of using a very sophisticated system of communication – language – to discuss feelings, ideas and possibilities. Premack (2004) points out that human intelligence is the only thing capable of doing science, producing new theories or explanations about the world and dealing with imaginary structures. No other animal on Earth has these capabilities. This raises the question of why humans are so different. Where did these abilities and high level of intelligence come from? The last two chapters considered animal intelligence; this chapter addresses questions about the evolution of human intelligence.

This chapter will cover:

- Evolution of modern humans
- Brain size
- Ecological factors
- Social factors
- Ecological dominance – social competition model
- Domain specific and domain general intelligence

Evolution of modern humans

Evolution is the gradual change in genetic material that eventually leads to new species. The changes over each generation tend to be very small but over hundreds of generations this leads to progressive changes that eventually lead to new species. These changes can be the result of genetic mutations caused during reproduction or of natural selection. Natural selection occurs when one feature, such as tooth structure, trunk size or brain size, gives a particular animal either a slight disadvantage or a slight advantage. Those with a slight advantage are more likely to survive and have offspring. Those with a slight disadvantage will tend to die out.

Humans are a species that are in a family called hominids, which includes both humans and the great apes. At some point in the past we shared common ancestors with the other great apes. These common ancestors lived in tropical forests and were mostly arboreal. When they did move between trees, they would normally walk on four limbs. Human evolution separated from that of the great apes about 6 million years ago. About 4 million years ago a line of species that are all called **hominins** began. Hominins are a group of species that include modern humans and their extinct ancestors (this group were called hominids but a recent reclassification of members of the hominoid family has resulted in a name change). They differ from the other great apes in a number of ways but the principal difference at first was that they were bipedal. Instead of normally walking on all four limbs they walked upright on their hind limbs. They also had larger brains than the great apes.

The increasingly big-brained hominins evolved into modern, highly intelligent humans in a very short time. This raises the question of why humans have evolved to be so intelligent so quickly. Unfortunately, 'intelligence' is shown in behaviour and this does not leave any direct evidence. To understand the evolution of intelligence we have to rely on other sources of evidence. One source is from fossil records. These give a number of important clues about hominin evolution and development of intelligence. The first is the size and shape of the skull. This gives clues to the development of the brain. It enables us to determine the size of the brain and to show which areas had increased or decreased in size (that is, information about the structure of the brain). Fossil records of other parts of the body can provide evidence of behaviour. For example, remains of hind limbs and pelvic region can help to determine whether a species was bipedal or not. Another source of evidence is from archaeology. Archaeological evidence shows whether particular groups were able to use tools, fire, art and so on.

Hominins and early *Homo sapiens* did not evolve in the conditions that modern humans live in. Their world was much more challenging; they had to struggle for food, shelter and safety. When considering what factors might have driven the evolution of hominins we have to be aware of the environment of our ancestors. We have to consider where they lived, how did they live and what pressures were there on the survival of both the species and the individual. As we investigate factors that might have influenced our evolution, we have to be aware of the **environment of evolutionary adaptation** (EEA). That is, we need to consider the conditions that shaped us at the time we evolved.

One of the first groups of hominins, the Australopithecines had brains not much bigger than chimps' (at about 400 cm^2 compared to 350 cm^2). One species, *Australopithecus afarensis* (the most famous of which is 'Lucy') appeared about 3.5 million years ago. This species was about the same size as a chimpanzee and was similar in appearance with long arms and short legs. However, the fossil remains of the legs and pelvis region suggest this species was bipedal. Furthermore there are fossilized footprints, found at Laetoli, Tanzania, which show that they walked on two legs. They probably did not walk like a modern human but more like a chimpanzee when they walk on their hind legs, with bent hips and knees.

About 2.5 million years ago there was a cooling of the Earth's climate. This resulted in a large reduction in the tropical forests and an increase in bush land and savannah. It also increased the seasonal changes in climate. At about this time one of the first Homo species, *Homo habilis* emerged. *Homo habilis* was adapted to living on open ground by being bipedal and by being more upright than the Australopithecines, thus increasing the field of vision. The teeth of this species suggest that they had a varied diet that included meat. There was also further enlargement and change to the organization of the brain. The changes included some enlargement of the frontal lobes and an increase in the number of gyri, which increased the neocortical area (Bailey and Geary, 2009). Archaeological evidence (cuts in animal bones) suggests that by about 2 million years ago *Homo habilis* were using crude stone tools.

About 2 million years ago there was a further cooling of the planet and the loss of more tropical forest. It is about this time that a different Homo species, *Homo ergastor* appeared. This species was tall, bipedal and had a narrow pelvis. The narrow pelvis makes bipedal movement much more effective but has a major disadvantage. A narrow pelvis makes giving birth more difficult, particularly to infants with large skulls. This shrinking of the pelvis may be why all later Homo species give birth to infants with an immature brain. This caused a change in behaviour, the immature brains of Homo infants meant that they required an extended period of care by their parents. Another development was that *Homo ergastor* developed better tools as they used well-shaped symmetrical hand axes.

About 1.8 million years ago species of Homo began to migrate out of Africa. For example, *Homo erectus* was found in Asia. This species used tools and discovered how to use and control fire. The brain size was about 75 per cent of that of a modern human. At roughly the same time, *Homo neanderthalensis* emerged in Europe and the Middle East. The Neanderthals, with a brain size roughly comparable to modern humans, seem to have been the first Homo species to deliberately bury their dead and may have had death rituals.

Modern humans, *Homo sapiens*, appeared about 200,000 to 150,000 years ago. Our species has a brain size of about 1350 cm^2, which is three to four times that of our early ancestors. Humans quickly learned how to make a variety of tools for different purposes (such as axes, knives and so on). *Homo sapiens* spread from Africa and by 40,000 years ago they were in the Middle East, Asia and Europe. This period is often referred to as the **Upper Palaeolithic Revolution**. This is because at this time there is evidence of cave art, jewellery making and figure carving. In other words there is an emergence of what we would regard as human culture. There is also evidence of more sophisticated hunting techniques. Soon after this other Homo species such as *erectus* and *neanderthalensis* became extinct and were replaced by *sapiens*. In a very short time, *Homo sapiens* have become a dominant species on the planet.

Summary

Humans come from a group of species called hominids, which includes humans and the great apes. The hominin line (humans and their ancestors) began diverging from the great apes about 6 million years ago. A defining feature of the hominin line is that they are bipedal and have adapted to live in bush land and savannah rather than being arboreal. Another feature of the hominin line is the rapid increase in brain size. One of the first hominins, *Australopithecus afarensis,* had a brain size that was only marginally larger than a chimpanzee's at 400 cm^2. Modern humans, *Homo sapiens*, have a brain size of 1350 cm^2. The rapid increase in the brain size in the Homo line has been accompanied by an increase in the sophistication of tools and the use of fire. *Homo sapiens* also developed art and culture.

Brain size and intelligence

The last section described how, over short period (in evolutionary terms), human brains tripled in size. This is a very rapid change to one organ and, although brain size is not necessarily an absolute indication of intelligence, it does help explain how humans have become so intelligent.

Humans do not have the largest brains. Large mammals such as elephants and whales have much larger brains (4 to 5 times of that of a human). However, it is evident that elephants are not more intelligent than humans. This is because the brain is not just involved in 'intelligent' activity but is needed to control all the physiological systems and muscles of the body. A large body requires more brain to control all these body processes. Absolute brain size is not a good measure of intelligence. A better measure is to look at the ratio of brain to body. A high ratio suggests there is more brain 'left over' from controlling the body for other, intelligent, functions. Humans have a high ratio (the brain is about 2 per cent of body) but not the highest.

Other measures include looking at the average ratio for a group of animals and then comparing individual species against the average. This gives the **encephalization quotient** (EQ). The average EQ is given a value of 1. Species that have a value lower than 1 have a lower brain size than expected, species with a value greater than 1 have a brain size greater than expected. Using this measure chimpanzees have an EQ of 2.5 suggesting their brains are more than twice the size expected of a mammal of similar size. Humans have an EQ of 7, which is the highest value of any species (Roth and Dicke, 2005). Compared with other mammals our brains are very large for our size. Even compared with other primates such as gorillas and chimpanzees human brains are three times larger when body weight is taken into consideration (Bailey and Geary, 2009)

The human brain is larger than that of its ancestors and relatives but not all the structures of the human brain have grown uniformly. Some areas of the human brain are relatively small compared to other mammals and even primates. For example, the olfactory areas are small which causes reduced sense of smell compared to other mammals. The cerebellum, which is involved in movement control and coordination, is smaller than might be expected of an animal our size. The biggest increase is in the frontal lobes of the cerebrum. There is some increase in all primate species but the increase is pronounced in humans. The frontal lobes are involved in planning and decision making (both of which are needed for 'intelligent' activities). Roth and Dicke (2005) point out that humans have a thick cortex which has a high cell density. Most of what we would regard as intelligent is processed in the cortex. The high number of cortical neurons enables humans to process information efficiently.

Large brains do have the advantage of enabling a species to have a high level of intelligence but there are drawbacks to having large brains. Firstly, brains are 'expensive'; they use more energy than any other organ. For example in humans, the brain makes up only 2 per cent of the body weight but uses 20 per cent of the body's energy (Roth and Dicke, 2005). Secondly, large brains need time to develop and infants are therefore completely dependent on parents. This affects survival chances of both infant and parents. Given these costs, the question is why there was such an investment in the development of a large brain in hominins. What drove the relatively rapid evolution of a large brain? There are a number of different theories of hominin brain evolution; some tend to concentrate on ecological factors and others on social factors.

Summary

Humans have a large brain. However, the human brain is not the largest and some large animals have a much larger brain. This is because the brain is needed to control the body's physiological processes and large animals need a larger brain to do so. A better measure to use in the comparison of brain size is the encephalization quotient (EQ). This compares the ratio of brain to body size for groups of animals. The average EQ is given a value of 1 and any value higher than this suggests a brain size higher than would be expected of a similar sized species. Humans have an EQ of 7, which is higher than any other species. The human brain has not developed uniformly and some structures have increased greatly while others are small compared to other species. Having a large brain does have significant drawbacks and this suggests there must be a good reason why they developed in hominins.

Ecological factors

There are a number of ecological factors that may have influenced the development of a large brain size and high intelligence in hominins. In the brief summary of human evolution, a number of these factors were mentioned. Many of them overlap but for convenience they have been separated into diet, foraging, the demands of being bipedal and climate.

Diet

As hominins moved from an arboreal existence to living on the ground their diet changed. The diet became much more diverse and required greater skill in both finding and obtaining food. The move to meat eating seen in the early Homo species provided a concentrated source of energy. This may have allowed the 'expensive' brain to develop.

The brain consumes a lot of energy but so do organs of the gastrointestinal tract. The 'expensive tissue hypothesis' (Aiello and Wheeler, 1995) suggests that any increase in brain size had to be balanced by a reduction in demands of these other expensive organs. The hypothesis suggests that the 'energy crisis' caused by an increase in brain size was solved by a reduction in gut size. This could only be achieved by increasing the nutritional value of the food. This hypothesis is supported by evidence that there is a significant positive correlation between diet quality and brain size in primates (Fish and Lockwood, 2003). Fish and Lockwood also found that evolutionary changes in diet are linked to changes in relative brain size. The evidence from both fossil and archaeological evidence suggests that meat played an increasingly important part of hominin diet from *Homo habilis* onwards.

Foraging demands

Species with complex foraging demands have larger brains and higher EQ values compared to related species with less complex foraging demands (Bailey and Geary, 2009). There is evidence that this may have played a part in hominin evolution. The diet for arboreal species tends to be leaves and fruit and in dense forest these are relatively abundant. On the other hand, food in bush land and savannah tends to be more scarce and dissipated. This requires more memory of different food sources to survive. In small groups, searching for food on the ground requires increased spatial awareness and coordination. The change from being arboreal to living in bush land and savannah increased both the range and the complexity of foraging. Bailey and Geary (2009) point out that changes in tooth structure and tool sophistication in early hominins are consistent with co-evolutionary changes in hunting efficiency, brain volume and EQ. However, King (1986) reviewed the role of extractive foraging in the evolution of primates. Extractive foraging is the locating and processing of embedded food (from the ground, from nuts and so on). King compared primates with other groups and concluded that extractive foraging played no significant role in the evolution of primate intelligence. King also concludes that it was a combination of factors (such as development of tools, division of labour and care of juveniles) that was important in the evolution of hominin intelligence rather than just foraging complexity.

Bipedal

Being bipedal may have evolved in hominins to increase the field of vision on open ground but it also had other advantages. Bipedalism leaves the arms free to hold and manipulate objects. The arms and hands can be used to use tools, to throw objects and to gesture. Fossil evidence shows a development of hands from Australopithecines onwards. All Homo species were able to precisely grip and manipulate objects and archaeological evidence shows an increasing sophistication of making and using tools from *Homo habilis* onwards. Aiello (1996) suggests that terrestiality and bipedalism are directly associated with an increase in brain size. This may be because of the cognitive demands of making, manipulating and using tools. Also the use of tools in hunting requires planning, decision making and many other cognitive functions that may be regarded as intelligent. However, it should be noted that humans are not the only bipedal species. Bipedalism is common among the marsupials in Australia yet this has not resulted in a very intelligent kangaroo.

Climate

Bailey and Geary (2009) note that climate variation can result from long-term changes that affect populations that do not migrate (for example ice ages) or from seasonal variations (particularly for hominin populations that migrated out of central Africa). Changes in climate both in the short and long term pose challenges to species. These challenges can be met either with physiological changes or with behavioural changes. Species, such as the hominins, that respond with changes to behaviour need to develop the intelligence to do so. Ash and Gallup (2007) studied the relationship between climate and change in brain size and EQ since the emergence of *Homo habilis*. They found that both brain size and EQ were correlated with the degree of seasonal temperature variation. They also found that brain size and EQ were correlated with distance from the equator. Since the temperature is cooler and more variable as distance from the equator increases, this supports the hypothesis that climate change may have influenced the evolution of intelligence.

Can ecological factors explain hominin intelligence?

Each of the ecological factors may have played a part in the evolution of human intelligence but each begs the question of how this is different to demands on other animals. Other species had changes in diet, other species changed from one environment to another, there are other bipedal species, others have had to deal with climatic variations and all species have been subject to various ecological demands. Why was it that *only* hominins had rapid change in brain size and intelligence? Not one of the ecological factors is unique to hominin EEA. Other researchers have looked at alternative factors and have questioned whether the answer to the evolution of hominin intelligence is more social.

Summary

Some theories of the evolution of hominin intelligence suggest that intelligence was the result of one or more changes to ecological factors. One of these is a change of diet. There is evidence that hominins changed from a fruit and seed diet to a more varied diet that included meat. Meat is a concentrated source of nutrients and energy and allows for the expansion of the 'expensive' brain. A second factor, related to diet, is change in foraging. As hominins moved from an arboreal existence to living on the open ground, foraging became more complex and demanding. The move to living on open ground introduced another factor, bipedalism. Being bipedal freed the arms of hominins for other tasks such as tool use. The making and using of tools increased the demands on cognitive abilities. A forth factor is climate. Both short-term seasonal changes and long-term trends in climate needed some response. One way of coping with climatic change is to change behaviour. This requires an increase in intelligence. One problem with all the ecological factors is that they are not unique to hominins. Thus they do not seem to answer the question of why it is only humans that have developed such a high level of intelligence.

Thinking scientifically →

Evolutionary psychology: A new paradigm?

Many of the theories about the evolution of intelligence discussed in this chapter have been put forward by evolutionary psychologists. Evolutionary psychology attempts to explain human behaviour (such as language, relationships, child care and so on) in evolutionary terms or as products of natural selection. Evolutionary psychologists argue that human behaviour can be understood as adaptations to the problems faced during hominin evolution (that is, in response to the EEA of our ancestors and early humans).

Two of the founders of evolutionary psychology, Tooby and Cosmides (2005, p. 5), describe it as:

> the long-forestalled scientific attempt to assemble out of the disjointed, fragmentary, and mutually contradictory human disciplines a single, logically integrated research framework for the psychological, social, and behavioural sciences – a framework that not only incorporates the evolutionary sciences on a full and equal basis, but that systematically works out all of the revisions in existing belief and research practice that such a synthesis requires.

Buss (1995) describes evolutionary psychology as a 'new paradigm' or a new way of viewing psychology. He suggests that this new paradigm has new conceptual tools for emerging from the current fragmented state of psychology and describes a number of principles that underpin the paradigm. A key one is that the human brain has specialized mechanisms that evolved to solve the adaptive problems of our hominin ancestors. Evolutionary psychologists use various sources of data for testing their hypotheses including archaeology, palaeontology, data from hunter-gatherer societies, observational studies, self-reports, and experimental studies of current human behaviour.

However this relatively new paradigm is not without critics or controversy. One of the critics is Buller (2005) who claims the current paradigm in evolutionary psychology has produced only questionable results. He claims there are a number of fallacies in the assumptions of evolutionary psychologists (Buller, 2009). A central problem is the assumption that an analysis of Pleistocene adaptive problems (the EEA) will yield clues to the mind's design. Buller suggests this key assumption is based on speculations about what those conditions were. Although we may have some clues about climate conditions, predators and so on, we have no information about social life, relationships or other critical features. He concludes:

> Of course, some speculations are worse than others. Those of Pop EP are deeply flawed. We are unlikely ever to learn much about our evolutionary past by slicing our Pleistocene history into discrete adaptive problems, supposing the mind to be partitioned into discrete solutions to those problems, and then supporting those suppositions with pencil-and-paper data. (Buller, 2009, p. 67)

Social factors

A second group of theories about the evolution of human intelligence focuses not on the ecological factors that might shape evolution but on social factors. Humans are a social species who live in groups. This introduces cognitive demands of relationships, communicating and competing in a social group. There are three (interrelated) social theories: social complexity, sexual selection and language.

Social complexity

Brain size in primates and some other animals such as cetaceans shows a positive correlation with size of the social group. The social complexity hypothesis is that the demands of living in larger groups led to selection for increased intelligence and brain size in humans (Dunbar, 1998). This is similar to the Machiavellian intelligence hypothesis but concentrates on the complexity of maintaining relationships in large groups. Although living in groups does have advantages (for hunting, protection from predators or rivals), it does also introduce some problems. For example, there can be competition between group members producing rivalry. Group members may need to form alliances to gain maximum advantage from group living. Living in a group requires an awareness of the relationship with others and an understanding of others. In other words, social relationships are complex. Flinn, Geary and Ward (2005) note that the potential variety of social puzzles in humans is infinite as no two social situations are identical. This requires high-level cognitive skills, or the development of intelligence. Furthermore, the variability of social interaction would favour the evolution of a system that was able to show general, rather than domain specific, intelligence (Geary, 2005). It is the high level of general intelligence shown by humans that appears to be different to other animals.

Bailey and Geary (2009) compared ecological, climate and social competition models of hominin brain evolution. They argue that if climatic and ecological pressures were the primary cause of brain evolution then factors such as climate and latitude should be the strongest predictor of variations in brain size. On the other hand, if social competition was the primary source then population density should be the strongest predictor. After reviewing various sources of evidence they conclude that multiple pressures drove hominin brain evolution but that the core selective force was social competition.

The social complexity hypothesis does not seem to explain why there was a rapid increase in intelligence in humans and not in other hominids. Dunbar (1993) suggests that this is because of group size. Hominids such as chimpanzees do not live in groups of more than 50 but in humans the typical group size was 150. Nevertheless, Flinn, Geary and Ward (2005) believe that the social complexity hypothesis encounters the same problems as the ecological hypotheses. That is, the hypothesis fails to answer the question of what is unique about hominin evolution. Flinn, Geary and Ward (2005, p. 13) suggest there are a number of unanswered questions such as:

> Given that hominin group size was unlikely to have been larger than that of their close relatives (the other hominoids), what was qualitatively different about the hominin social environment? Why did hominins, in particular, form more socially complex groups, hence creating an environment in which more sophisticated forms of social cognition (for example, TOM) and general intelligence would have been more strongly favoured by natural selection than in related species? Why were coalitions more important, and more cognitively taxing, for our hominin ancestors than for any other species in the history of life?

Thus, although the social complexity hypothesis may be more satisfactory than the ecological theories, it does not provide a complete answer to the conundrum of why humans developed great intelligence so quickly.

Sexual selection

The idea that sexual selection was responsible for the evolution of human intelligence was first put forward by Darwin (1871). He speculated that mental prowess was analogous to the peacock's tail in that it influenced mate choice. This hypothesis was revised by Miller (2000) who believes that mate choice for increasingly intelligent mates by hominins was an important selection pressure that led to the rapid increase in intelligence. The hypothesis suggests that the choice of intelligent mates caused a positive feedback loop which resulted in ever increasing brain size and intelligence. Like the peacock's tail, a large brain did not have value in itself (indeed it imposed costs on the individual by using 20 per cent of the energy intake) but it did improve reproductive success. Miller suggests that the evolution of intelligence and a large brain was less about survival during the day and more about courtship problems hominins faced at night.

Miller (2000) also believes that the emergence of culture, including art and music, is a result of this sexual selection. Activities such as art and music have no survival value to an individual and it is a puzzle how they became such an intrinsic part of human culture. Miller suggests such activities were signs of intelligence and creativity and individuals showing these abilities would be selected as mates. Miller therefore implies that the source of the traits we think of as being typically human have come to be built into our character during the evolutionary history in which hominins chose sexual partners on the basis of intelligence and creativity.

Flinn, Geary and Ward (2005) believe that, although mate choice may have had a significant effect, it is unclear why hominins were the only group of species where sexual selection was made on mental capabilities.

Language

Humans are a highly intelligent species but they have one other feature that sets them apart, the use of language (Lund, 2003). As noted in the previous chapter, it may be possible to teach some primates the rudiments of language but none learn it to the same degree or with the ease that humans do. Language is a highly complex system of communication that is cognitively very demanding. It requires the manipulation of abstract symbols (words) using complex rules (grammar) to convey elaborate and subtle ideas. Language takes years to learn in infancy and needs specific areas of the brain to both produce and understand it. This raises the question of whether it was the development of language that led to the need for increased in intelligence in hominins. To answer this, two questions need to be addressed; firstly, when did language develop and secondly (and more importantly), why did language develop?

The question of when did language develop is a difficult one to answer. Although the fossil records can show when the shape of the bones in the throat could possibly be used to produce language-like sounds, there is no evidence that the hominins actually did so. Barrett, Dunbar and Lycett (2002) suggest there are at least three views of the origin of language. One is that it evolved very early, perhaps with *Homo erectus* as much as 1.5 million years ago. The second is that it evolved with the emergence of *Homo sapiens.* The third is that it is a comparatively recent development linked to the Upper Palaeolithic Revolution about 50,000 years ago. Barrett, Dunbar and Lycett (2002) cast doubt on the possibility that language developed very early but note that there is some evidence that is consistent with language emerging with early *Homo sapiens.* Language requires very fine control of the muscles used to control breathing. Modern humans have an expansion in the spinal cord in the thoracic region to accommodate the nerves needed to do this. This increase is found in the earliest *Homo sapiens* fossils. However, there is evidence that a crucial area for language in modern humans, Broca's area, developed long before *Homo sapiens* (Harley, 2001). Aiello and Dunbar (1993) believe we should view language evolution as being in three stages: an early content-less form of vocal grooming with *Homo erectus*, a social content phase in early *Homo sapiens* and a modern phase involving symbolic meaning after the Upper Palaeolithic Revolution.

There are two types of theory as to why language developed. The first is that language evolved for information exchange or instruction. This view is that the information transmitted by language would aid activities such as hunting and make it more efficient. Barrett, Dunbar and Lycett (2002) point out that there are flaws in this view. Studies of modern hunter-gatherers suggest that far from being useful in hunting, speech is kept to a minimum. Also, studies of the way humans use language show we do not use it much for information exchange. The vast majority of language is for social use; we use language to gossip. The second type of theory focuses on this social aspect of language. This view is that, as social groups of hominins grew larger, they needed a more efficient way of achieving group cohesion and maintaining relationships. Language fulfils this function and becomes a form of 'social grooming' (Dunbar,

1997). Most social animals need some mechanism to maintain group harmony and in primates that mechanism is grooming. The time devoted to grooming increases as the group size increases (Dunbar, 1993). No primate species spends more than 20 per cent of their waking hours grooming and this limits the group size to about 50. However, *Homo* species had a typical group size of 150. If they relied on grooming to maintain cohesion it is estimated it would have taken a disproportionate amount, perhaps up to 40 per cent, of their waking time. This would severely limit the time available for foraging for food and finding water and shelter. Barrett, Dunbar and Lycett (2002) suggest that human populations were able to become larger because of the development of language. Language enables humans to interact with many individuals at the same time. Gossiping became our means of maintaining group cohesion and a highly effective replacement for grooming.

Aiello and Dunbar (1993) link the evolution of language to group size and neocortex size. The need for efficient social communication within a large group led to language, which in turn led to an increase in neocortex. The increase in the neocortex made humans more intelligent. Premack (2004) asks whether language is the key to human intelligence. He notes that while other animals may be able to learn by imitation only humans can teach by using language. Human language is very flexible and this may be one reason we are able to solve problems and use imagination or, to be intelligent.

The argument that large group size and development of language led to increased intelligence does leave some questions. The main question remains – why did these factors affect hominins only? If the hypothesis is that better communication (and eventually language) developed to cope with increased group size in hominins then the question 'why did group size increase?' arises. In other words there seems to be a question of cause and effect. Did language develop to cope with increased group size or did group size increase because communication improved?

Summary

The failure of ecological theories to explain the unique development of intelligence in hominins led to theories that focused on social factors. The social complexity theory is that as group size increased it increased the complexity of relationships within the group. This in turn required an increase in intelligence to deal with the cognitive demands made by living in a large group. However, it is not clear why this should occur in hominins but not other primates. The sexual selection hypothesis is that mate choice for increasingly intelligent mates by hominins led to the rapid increase in intelligence. Thus intelligence and creativity led to reproductive success. Again, it is not clear why intelligence should be selected as the basis of mate choice in only the hominin line. Language is a complex communication system that requires a great deal of cognitive processing. It is possible that the rapid increase in intelligence seen in hominins was the result of the demands of using language. One theory focuses on the social aspects of language and suggests that as hominin group size increased, social cohesion could not be maintained by grooming. Language, and therefore intelligence, developed as a more effective means of achieving group cohesion and maintaining relationships. As with the social cohesion hypothesis, this theory does not explain why this happened in hominins only.

Ecological dominance–social competition model

Each of the ecological and social theories above has problems in explaining the evolution of human intelligence alone. Each one provides a partial explanation of why humans went through a rapid evolution of intelligence and brain size but none fully explain it. As Flinn, Geary and Ward (2005, p. 10) note:

> hypotheses based on traditional ecological demands, such as hunting or climatic variability, have not provided satisfying explanations. Recent models based on social problem solving linked with ecological conditions offer more convincing scenarios. But it has proven difficult to identify a set of selective pressures that would have been sufficiently unique to the hominin lineage.

The phrase 'sufficiently unique to the hominin lineage' is a key one: the discussion of the various theories above show that none of them *by themselves* are unique to hominins. The problem with each theory is that it seems to be only part of the answer. The focus on ecological factors or social factors may miss the broad picture of the hominin EEA. It is possible that the evolution of hominin intelligence was the result of a unique *combination* of selective pressures. One attempt to integrate a variety of factors is the 'ecological dominance–social competition' or EDSC model (Alexander, 1989).

The EDSC model proposes that hominin evolution is unique because an early increase in intelligence allowed them to begin to overcome ecological pressures. The use of tools and the ability to throw meant hominins achieved some degree of ecological dominance. This meant they used resources better, resulting in a reduction in mortality and an increase in population size. As a result of the increase in population size, the evolutionary pressure came from inter- and intra-group competition and cooperation. The rapid evolution in intelligence occurred because hominins became 'their own principal hostile force of nature' (Alexander, 1989, p. 469). Hominins had to develop sophisticated cognitive abilities, including social skills and language, to enable them to compete with other hominins. We developed large brains not to deal with ecological pressures but to deal with other large brains! The more intelligent were able to survive and reproduce. Flinn, Geary and Ward (2005, p. 11) suggest this amounted to an 'autocatalytic social arms race'. Unlike the static demands of ecological factors, this form of selection was thus based on relative rather than absolute intelligence. This results in an upward spiral of intelligence.

Flinn, Geary and Ward (2005, p. 35) believe the model is supported by a 'unique combination of coevolved characteristics and their temporal sequencing'. For example, hominins have an unusual pattern of evolution in that only modern humans (*Homo sapiens*) remain from the evolutionary line. The human neocortex is larger in areas that support uniquely human social skills such as language and ToM. Humans have an unusual reproductive pattern with extended childhoods and post-reproductive stages. Flinn, Geary and Ward (2005) claim that these, and many other features that are unique to humans, can only be explained by the existence of social competition in the context of increasing ecological dominance.

They also note that the foci of human mental processing are unusual. Most species have evolved cognitive specializations to deal with specific ecological problems or some specialized social problems. Humans have evolved cognitive abilities to deal with sophisticated social problems and have developed language, ToM, empathy, love and so on. Such social abilities, rather than being 'additional' skills, occupy most of our thoughts. Indeed, they argue that it is the advantages that these cognitive skills gave for dealing with ecological demands that were secondary. Spink and Cole

(2007) claim the EDSC model currently provides the most comprehensive theory about the evolution of human socio-cognitive abilities.

Summary

The EDSC model proposes that early increases in hominin intelligence allowed them to begin to overcome ecological pressures. Hominins achieved a degree of ecological dominance which resulted in lower mortality and a higher population. As a result, the evolutionary pressure came from inter- and intra-group competition and cooperation. Hominins had to develop ever increasingly complex cognitive abilities to compete and cooperate with other hominins. In effect, ecological dominance resulted in a mental arms race where the selection was made on the basis of intelligence. Intelligence evolved primarily for social reasons but it also enabled further dominance of ecological pressures. It is argued that this theory is able to explain a number of features that are unique to humans and their evolution.

Domain specific and domain general intelligence

In this chapter, intelligence has been discussed as a single, general characteristic. However, many psychologists recognize that there are various types of intelligence. One distinction is between domain specific and domain general intelligence (Chiappe and MacDonald, 2005). Domain specific intelligences are forms of intelligence that have evolved to deal with specific problems or demands. Most animals have evolved sets of specific problem-solving skills to deal with the demands of their environment. For example, Clark's nutcracker (a type of crow found in America) has evolved the ability to remember where it has stored thousands of seeds in order to survive the winter when no fresh food is available. Humans, living in large social groups, have the ability to recognize thousands of other human faces. Domain general intelligence is the ability to use intelligence to solve novel problems. It has not evolved to deal with a specific environmental problem but to deal with many different problems. This type of general intelligence is evident in most human activity (see the discussion of general intelligence, *g*, in Chapter 6).

Cosmides and Tooby (2002) believe that one of the enigmas of human intelligence is why and how have we developed this domain general intelligence. Evolutionary psychology provides a good explanation about why and how domain specific abilities developed in animals and humans but, as Chiappe and MacDonald (2005) point out, ideas from evolutionary psychology seems at odds with the existence of domain generality in human intelligence. When the EEA presents recurrent problems then an optimal solution is to evolve domain specific mechanisms (or intelligences) to deal with them. However, it is hard to imagine a specific problem in the human EEA that might lead to the evolution of domain general. Chiappe and MacDonald (2005) believe that the key to the development of domain general intelligence was the variety of rapidly changing ecological conditions in hominin evolution. This period of rapid change saw the appearance and disappearance of a number of hominin species. Chiappe and MacDonald (2005) suggest the key to survival during this period was the development of mechanisms designed to deal with novel and unpredictable problems, in other words, domain general intelligence.

Further reading

Flinn, M.V., Geary, D.C. and Ward, C.V. (2005) Ecological dominance, social competition, and coalitionary arms races: Why humans evolved extraordinary intelligence. *Evolution and Human Behavior,* 26, 10–46.

Geary, D.C. (2005) *The Origins of Mind: Evolution of Brain, Cognition and General Intelligence.* Washington, DC: American Psychological Association.

Sternberg, R.J. and Kaufman, N.J. (eds) (2002) *The Evolution of Intelligence*. Mahwah, NJ: Lawrence Erlbaum Associates.

Chapter 6

Theories of intelligence

There is no doubt that, as a species, *Homo sapiens* are intelligent. During the course of our recent evolution we have evolved to have large brains and a very high EQ. Humans are a hugely inventive species that are able to solve complex problems. It is also evident that humans show intelligence in different spheres; some are gifted linguists, some are excellent musicians while others are talented in sport. The term intelligence potentially covers a wide range of possible activities and abilities. This makes it difficult to pinpoint what it is that constitutes intelligence. For example, it could include verbal abilities, numerical abilities, reasoning and social skills or none of these. In a review of the nature of intelligence, Carroll (1993) identified over 70 different abilities that were being assessed by various forms of intelligence tests. The complexity of concept and the question of what is human intelligence were examined briefly in Chapter 1 by exploring the layperson's view. This chapter is concerned with psychologists' theories of intelligence.

This chapter will cover:

- Psychometric theories of intelligence
- Gardner's theory of multiple intelligences
- Information-processing approach: Anderson's theory of minimal cognitive architecture
- Information-processing approach: Sternberg's triarchic theory of intelligence
- Emotional intelligence

Psychometric theories of intelligence

The psychometric approach

Psychometrics is concerned with the measurement of psychological variables. There are two aspects of the psychometric approach: the construction of tests to measure a variable and the development of theory about the measurements.

The psychometric approach to intelligence assumes that intelligence can be measured and that there are individual differences in the level of intelligence. The first intelligence tests were developed by Binet and Simon in 1905 to assess which children might need special education. These early tests consisted of items that ranged in difficulty. When given to children of different ages the older children were able to do more of the tasks than the younger children. Binet and Simon were able to establish norms for each age group. These norms represented a 'mental age', or what a child should be capable of at a given age. This could be used to assess whether a child was advanced or backward for their age. For example, if a 5-year-old child showed a mental age of 6 then they would be doing better than the norm for their age. However, if a 6-year-old child showed a mental age of 5 then they would be behind the norm for their age.

This concept was used by Stern in 1911 to develop the concept of an **intelligence quotient** or IQ. Stern noticed that the mental age of children varied proportionately to their age. If a child of 5 showed a mental age of $4\frac{1}{2}$, by the time they were 10 their mental age was typically 9. The difference between chronological and mental age was not absolute but was a ratio. Stern therefore suggested that the ratio of mental and chronological age should be used to quantify intelligence. He defined his new measure IQ as the mental age divided by the chronological age times a 100. Thus the average IQ is 100 since the mental age is the norm for a particular age group.

In 1939 Wechsler published some tests that had been standardized on adults and in 1955 he introduced two tests, one for children and the other for adults. Versions of both tests, the Wechsler Intelligence Scale for Children (WISC) and the Wechsler Adult Intelligence Scale (WAIS) are still used. Both tests have subtests that are designed to measure different aspects of intelligence such as arithmetic, comprehension, digit span, picture arrangement, vocabulary and so on. Some of these are verbal tests and some are performance tests. The introduction of adult tests led to a problem with the concept of IQ. Although the ratio of mental and chronological age worked as a basis for IQ in children, it does not with adults. As adults age chronologically, their mental age may not increase. Using Stern's method of calculating IQ this would suggest their IQ decreases each year. For example, a 20 year old with a mental age of 20 would have an IQ of 100. However if their mental age stayed the same, by the time they were 30 their IQ would be 67 and by 40 their IQ would be 50! Wechsler's answer was to calculate IQ by using a normal distribution. He noticed that when the adult scales were given to a large number of people there was a normal distribution of scores (that is, a few people had very low scores, a lot of people had medium scores and a few had very high scores). He took 100 as being the average score (since Stern had established this figure as the average). The normal distribution curve can then be used to show how a particular individual's score compares to others. If their score is average they have an IQ of 100, if higher then they have a higher than average IQ and if lower, they have a lower than average IQ. Wechsler used standard deviations to determine scores. One standard deviation represented 15 IQ points, which means that the majority of adults (68 per cent) have IQs that fall between 85 and 115.

One criticism of the Wechsler scales is that they seem to measure knowledge and memory rather than the ability to solve new problems. Raven introduced a different measure, Raven's progressive matrices, in 1938. The progressive matrices are designed to measure abstract reasoning and non-verbal abilities.

Factor theories of intelligence

Many of the early theories of intelligence were based on factor analysis of intelligence tests given to many participants. These theories are therefore based on the psychometric approach. Factor analysis is a statistical technique that is used to find out which tests or kinds of questions have strong links to each other and which do not. The technique therefore investigates correlations between tests. A strong correlation would be found if some individuals scored highly in all tests and others had low scores in all tests. Tests or items that are strongly correlated would appear to be measuring the same thing; or a factor. However, factor analysis is a complicated technique that can be done in various ways. As a result, one researcher may find few factors but another may find many. The first theory to be examined, Spearman's, suggests that intelligence had few dimensions or factors.

Spearman's theory

Spearman (1923) was one of the first to propose a factor theory of intelligence. He based his theory on factor analysis of a number of tests given to children over a long period of time. Analysis of this mass of data suggested that there were positive correlations between the various tests: individuals who did well on one test tended to do well on the others, conversely those that did poorly on one tended to do poorly on all. This led him to propose a two factor theory of intelligence. The first factor was specific abilities, or 's'. This was the name given to the ability to do each type of test (such as verbal ability or mathematical ability). These specific abilities were positively correlated with each other. However, Spearman's theory is best known for the second factor which was called **general intelligence** or **'*g*'**. Spearman argued that *g* was the underlying ability that determined a person's level of intelligence. Thus *g* was the underlying intelligence that led to the specific abilities. He envisaged *g* as a form of mental energy that drove the intellect. Spearman assumed that a high *g* meant that person was intelligent in all specific abilities.

The notion of *g* has been debated ever since and is one of the most influential ideas in psychology. The idea of a single factor or *g* behind intelligence is still held by a number of psychologists but many others now feel that a single factor cannot represent the complexity and diversity of human intelligence. Another problem with the theory is that the statistical technique of factor analysis can be interpreted in a number of ways. The data can be seen as pointing to one factor or can be interpreted as showing that intelligence consists of many factors

Thurstone's theory

Like Spearman, Thurstone (1938) used factor analysis to analyse the results of many intelligence tests (56 tests to 240 students). However Thurstone argued that the evidence from his analysis suggested that intelligence consisted of seven primary mental abilities, rather than one general factor, *g*. He argued that the primary mental abilities taken together resulted in an overall level of intelligence. Thurstone described the seven primary abilities as:

1 Verbal comprehension – the ability to understand written and spoken information

2. Verbal fluency – the ability to generate verbal material rapidly
3. Number – the ability to perform mathematical operations
4. Perceptual speed – the speed of recognizing perceptual stimuli
5. Spatial realization – the ability to mentally manipulate shapes and objects
6. Memory – the ability to remember different types of material
7. Inductive reasoning – the ability to generate conclusions from information

Thurstone did not include '*g*' as one of his primary abilities but he did note that his seven primary abilities did show a positive correlation between each other. Later researchers have suggested that a factor analysis of the primary abilities could produce a general factor (Sternberg, 1985).

Cattell's theory

Cattell (1971) was another person who used factor analysis. He agreed with Spearman that there was some form of general intelligence but he suggested there are two separate components: **crystallized intelligence** and **fluid intelligence**. Crystallized intelligence (or 'Gc') is the type of intelligence that uses stored knowledge and skills. Thus the accumulation of vocabulary, general knowledge and specific knowledge are all part of crystallized intelligence. Fluid intelligence (or 'Gf') is the type of intelligence used when dealing with novel situations (that is, it does not require stored knowledge). This type is linked to the ability to reason, to solve abstract problems and to acquire new understanding.

Cattell argued that Gc depends on Gf, since fluid intelligence allows us to accumulate new knowledge, which becomes part of crystallized. He also suggests that Gc increases throughout life since it is the accumulation of learning. However Gf changes over time, gradually increasing in childhood before stabilizing in adulthood and declining in later years. However, this is not supported by some empirical evidence. For example, Schaie (1996) carried out a longitudinal study of intelligence in adults from the age of 53 to 81 and found that the decline in fluid intelligence was only slightly more than the decline in crystallized intelligence.

Hierarchical models

Spearman suggested that intelligence is best described using one general factor, *g*. Thurstone on the other hand suggested intelligence consists of seven primary abilities. Hierarchical models suggest that a synthesis of the two views provides a better account of the nature of intelligence. The two prominent hierarchical models, that of Vernon and Carroll, both suggest that intelligence consists of a general intelligence at the top of the hierarchy with primary group abilities beneath. However, they differ on the detail.

Vernon (1971) suggests that intelligence is composed of various abilities that are grouped at four levels arranged in a hierarchy (see Figure 6.1). The most important ability, general intelligence (similar to *g*) is at the top of the hierarchy. Vernon believed that *g* encompassed two major group factors which he put at the next level. These two major group factors are verbal/educational (v:ed) and spatial/mechanical intelligence (k:m). The major group factor v:ed represents verbal intelligence and the ability to manipulate and understand verbal and numerical material whereas k:m represents the ability to mentally manipulate shapes. The next level on the hierarchy consists of minor group factors that make up the major group factors. For example, under the major group factor v:ed there are minor group factors such as verbal, numerical and educational factors. At the bottom of the hierarchy are the specific intelligence factors that make up the minor group factors. For example, under the verbal minor group factor there are specific factors such as comprehension, reading, use of grammar and so on.

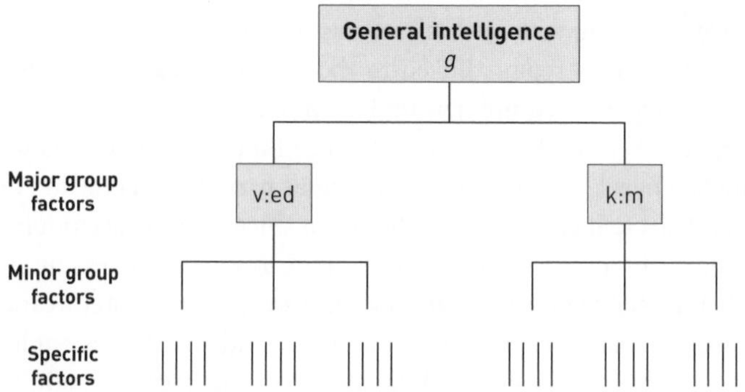

Figure 6.1 Vernon's model of intelligence

The second hierarchical model, proposed by Carroll (1997), is called the Three-Stratum Model of Human Cognitive Abilities (see Figure 6.2). Like Vernon, Carroll suggested that the top layer of the hierarchy, which he calls stratum 3, is a general level of intelligence similar to *g*. However, instead of suggesting that this could be divided into two major group factors, Carroll proposed the next layer, stratum 2, consisted of eight broad factors. These include: fluid intelligence (Gf), crystallized intelligence (Gc), general memory and learning (Gy), broad cognitive speediness (Gs), broad visual perception (Gv), broad auditory perception (Gu), broad retrieval ability (Gr) and processing speed (Gt). The bottom level, stratum 1, represents specific factors that make up the broad factors.

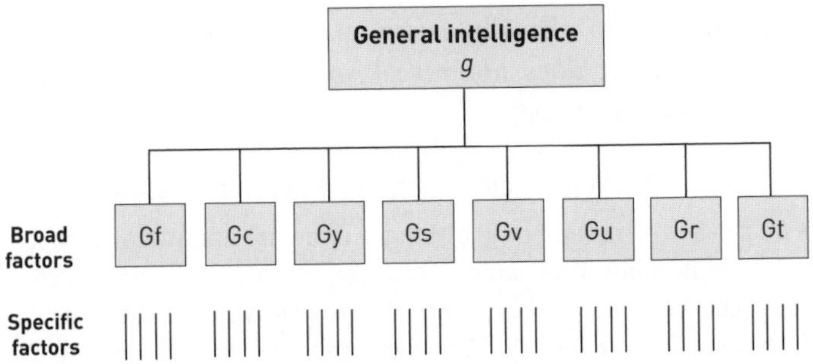

Figure 6.2 The Three-Stratum Model of Human Cognitive Abilities

Carroll's model brings together many elements from previous researchers. He includes the notion of *g* introduced by Spearman and the notion of broad factors introduced by Thurstone. The model also embraces the concepts of crystallized and fluid intelligence that were proposed by Cattell. Finally, like Vernon, Carroll has described these various forms of intelligence in a hierarchical structure.

Can factor analysis identify intelligence?

All the theories above use factor analysis to establish what factors constitute intelligence. However, factor analysis has a number of problems. One of the major problems of factor analysis is that it describes the links within a mass of data about intelligence but cannot explain it. As Mackintosh (1998, p. 230) points out 'Factor analysis can do no more than describe the relationship between different IQ tests. This is not the same as uncovering the structure of human abilities'. Secondly, the results from factor analysis are only as good as the data that it is used to analyse. If the data is unreliable or invalid then the results of the factor analysis become invalid. Thirdly, even if the data that is analysed is valid the factors revealed from factor analysis depend on data put in. Eysenck (2004) uses a sausage machine analogy; you can only get out of factor analysis what you put in. Thus, if none of the data going in relates to creativity, then no factor of 'creativity' can emerge from the factor analysis. Similarly if no data about emotional sensitivity, interpersonal relationships and so on is included they cannot emerge as a factor. Thus the factors found are predetermined by the factors put into the data. As Sternberg, Lautrey and Lubart (2002, p. 6) point out 'factor analysis provides simply a psychometric transformation of what one puts in'. Finally, factor analysis relies on interpretation of the analysis, it does not reveal an 'answer' (see 'Thinking scientifically – Factor analysis').

Thinking scientifically → **Factor analysis**

Factor analysis is a method of analysing a large set of data to extract factors from a number of variables. However, it is a complicated technique that can be done in many ways. In an evaluation of the use of factor analysis in psychology, Fabrigar, Wegener, MacCallum, and Strahan (1999) point out that researchers need to make a number of design and analytical decisions when using the technique and that each decision has important consequences for the result of the analysis. These decisions include which type of technique to use, the factor extraction procedure and how many factors are extracted from the analysis. Fabrigar et al. suggest that the decisions made in the design and analysis when using factor analysis are frequently the wrong ones.

Gardner, Kornhaber and Wake (1996, p. 69) point out that 'there are defensible and reasonable ways to proceed in factor analysis, but there is no single mathematical correct solution to a factor analysis'. They note that most researchers rotate the factors to find factors that are more highly associated. This can be done in a number of ways and then has to be interpreted. As Sternberg (1977) points out, each orientation is equally acceptable mathematically and that factorial theories differed because of orientations as much as anything else.

Researchers tend to use rules of thumb or heuristics to interpret results so even if data is factored in the same way there is more than one interpretation.

All statistical analysis needs to be interpreted but with factor analysis there is no single way of obtaining factors or one single answer to the analysis. The 'answer' depends on the decisions made throughout the analysis and then the interpretation of that analysis.

Summary

The psychometric approach to intelligence assumes that intelligence differs among individuals and that this difference can be measured by tests. The first intelligence test was developed for children by Binet and Simon and was used to establish the mental age of children. Stern used the idea of mental age to develop a measure of intelligence which he called intelligence quotient (IQ). This is essentially a ratio of mental and chronological age. Wechsler developed intelligence tests for both children and adults. The original method of calculating IQ did not work on adult populations therefore Wechsler used the normal distribution curve and standard deviations to determine adult IQ.

A number of theories about the nature of intelligence have emerged from using a statistical technique called factor analysis. One of the first to use this technique, Spearman proposed that intelligence was governed by one general actor of intelligence, or *g*. Thurstone on the other hand suggested that intelligence was best viewed as comprising seven primary abilities rather than a single factor. Cattell agreed that there was a general intelligence but believed that this was divided into crystallized and fluid intelligence. Hierarchical models, such as Carroll's Three-Stratum Model of Human Cognitive Abilities, suggest intelligence is composed of both a general intelligence factor and broad intelligence factors arranged in a hierarchy. Factor analysis may be a useful way of establishing the factors that make up intelligence but there are some problems with the technique. Factor analysis provides a way of grouping factors but does not provide an explanation of intelligence, and the factors that emerge depend entirely on the data analysed.

Gardner's theory of multiple intelligences

Gardner (1983) put forward his theory of multiple intelligences in challenge to what he calls traditional view in intelligence. This view is based on capacity for abstract reasoning and verbal abilities and still links to the notion of *g* (Gardner, Kornhaber and Wake, 1996). Gardner did not agree with the notion a single general intelligence. He based his theory on a wide range of sources rather than just the traditional psychometric test data. He used such data but in addition looked at evidence from neuropsychology. Neuropsychology investigates the selective impairments to abilities caused by brain damage. Some such patients may show problems with verbal abilities but still have excellent spatial skills, others may show the reverse. He also looked at evidence from **savants** who typically have a low IQ but excel at one ability or another (music, drawing and so on). In addition he examined findings from a wide range of psychological studies. Gardner analysed and synthesized the evidence from these diverse sources to suggest a theory of multiple intelligences. Each 'intelligence' is used as a term for describing human capabilities rather than a thing to be measured (or 'some commodity inside the head', Gardner, Kornhaber and Wake, 1996, p. 205). Gardner also suggested that each type of intelligence has a biological underpinning and describes each one as a biopsychological potential to process information (Gardner, 2006). Rather than using factor analysis to categorize aspects of intelligence, Gardner (1983) used a number of criteria to identify different types of intelligence. These criteria include:

1. The intelligence should depend upon identifiable brain structures.
2. There should be evidence of the intelligence from neuropsychology. Some brain-damaged individuals should show impairment in one type of intelligence but not in others.
3. There should be individuals who show outstanding abilities or deficits linked to the intelligence type.
4. The intelligence should show some evolutionary history.
5. The intelligence should use specific cognitive operations.
6. There should be support for the intelligence from appropriate psychological tests.

Based on these criteria, Gardner originally proposed seven forms of intelligence. The first two are linked to the traditional view of intelligence and are typically valued in education; the next three are normally associated with the arts; and the last two are linked to personal intelligence (Gardner, 1999). These seven types are:

1. *Linguistic intelligence*. This involves both spoken (listening and speaking) and written (reading and writing) language. It includes the ability to learn languages and to be able to use language to express ideas. The ability to use language to remember information is also part of this intelligence. Gardner suggests this intelligence is exemplified by poets.

2 *Logical-mathematical intelligence*. This consists of the ability to analyse abstract problems and to perform mathematical operations. It also includes the ability to reason and think logically. It is most often associated with scientific and mathematical thinking and is exemplified by scientists.
3 *Musical intelligence*. This is involved in both producing music (composition and performance) and in appreciation of music. It includes the capacity to recognize elements such as pitch and rhythm. It is exemplified by composers.
4 *Bodily-kinaesthetic intelligence*. This is involved in the fine control of movement of either part of the body or the whole body. It is the use of mental abilities to coordinate the body to solve physical problems and is exemplified by dancers or sportspersons.
5 *Spatial intelligence*. This is the ability to perceive and mentally modify spatial information.
6 *Intrapersonal intelligence*. This is concerned with the ability to understand oneself and includes the capacity to recognize one's own motivations and feelings. It is the self-knowledge that allows people to build an accurate mental model of themselves.
7 *Interpersonal intelligence*. This is concerned with the capacity to understand other people. It is the ability to recognize the feelings, intentions and motivations of others.

Gardner (1998) later added an eighth intelligence to the theory: naturalistic intelligence. This is concerned with the ability to recognize and categorize patterns in nature. He also speculated about another two, spiritual intelligence and existential intelligence, but did not feel there was sufficient evidence to include them as separate intelligences.

Gardner regards each type of intelligence as being independent of the others and not under the influence of a general intelligence. However, Gardner, Kornhaber and Wake (1996) note that an important point is that people draw on combinations of them in demonstrating intelligent behaviour. For example, a dancer might use primarily bodily-kinaesthetic intelligence but may need musical intelligence and the personal intelligences to give a good performance. Gardner (1999) also suggests that each person has a unique blend of the different types of intelligence.

Do multiple intelligences exist?

Gardner (1983, p. 70) regards the multiple intelligences 'only as potentially useful scientific constructs'. Nevertheless, the theory has generated much interest and debate. Eysenck (2004) claims that despite the popularity of Gardner's theory there is little direct evidence to support it. One source of evidence comes from a study of creativity by Gardner (1993) using case studies of famous individuals of the twentieth century. Each individual was chosen to epitomize one of seven original intelligences. For example, Einstein was used to epitomize logical-mathematical intelligence, Stravinsky was used for musical intelligence, Gandhi was used for interpersonal intelligence and so on. Gardner found that there were great similarities in the upbringing and attitudes of all seven individuals. However, Eysenck (2004) points out that had different individuals been chosen to illustrate each type of intelligence these similarities would disappear. A different way of examining the theory is to explore the criteria Gardner used to identify different types of intelligence. Gardner, Kornhaber and Wake (1996) point to such evidence for each type of intelligence. For example, there is a variety of evidence for a linguistic intelligence. Neuropsychological data shows that brain-damaged individuals can have great difficulties in either producing or understanding speech but suffer no impairment to other abilities. Studies from neuroscience have revealed a variety of dedicated mechanisms linked to language production and comprehension. There are individuals who show remarkable linguistic skills but do not show high intelligence in other spheres (for example Williams syndrome). However, Eysenck (2004) notes that there are other skills that meet the criteria, such as face perception, which are not regarded as a type of intelligence.

The theory has also been criticized on other grounds. For example, Scarr (1985) claims that the labelling of various skills as intelligences is socially motivated rather than scientifically based. Scarr (1989) further suggests that the theory confuses intelligence with other human characteristics. Anderson (1992) agrees and believes that the multiple intelligences are ill defined. He claims that, rather than being intelligences, they are sometimes a behaviour and sometimes a cognitive process. In the American Psychological Association (APA) task force report on intelligence, Neisser et al. (1996, p. 79) point out that critics of the theory argue that some of the types of intelligence described by Gardner 'are more appropriately described as special talents than as forms of "intelligence"'.

The idea that the seven (now eight) intelligences are autonomous has also been criticized. If they are separate and independent then there should be no correlation between the different types. However, most research shows that there are positive correlations between different abilities and that no individual capacity is wholly independent from others. For example, Visser, Ashton and Vernon (2006) investigated Gardner's theory using two tests for each type of intelligence with 200 adults. They found strong links between linguistic, logical/mathematical, spatial, naturalistic and interpersonal intelligences which they suggest shows a *g* factor. They found weaker links with other types and believe they resemble the group factors in hierarchical models.

Although the theory has not been readily accepted by some academic psychologists, it has had an impact on education, particularly in the USA. The use in schools varies but in general they all attempt to help children draw on a range of their intelligences. However, evidence about the impact of school programmes based on the theory remains inconclusive. Sternberg and Kaufman (1998, p. 493) conclude 'many of the programs are unevaluated, and evaluation of others of these programs seem to be ongoing'.

Summary

Gardner rejected the traditional notion of a general intelligence and using evidence from a wide range of sources put forward a theory of multiple intelligences. He originally suggested that there are seven, independent forms of intelligence. These are linguistic intelligence, logical-mathematical intelligence, musical intelligence, bodily-kinaesthetic intelligence, spatial intelligence, intrapersonal intelligence and interpersonal intelligence. He later added naturalistic intelligence to the original seven. Gardner's theory has generated much interest and debate. Although there is some supporting evidence from neuropsychology and case studies, there are doubts about the validity of the various intelligences. In particular there is uncertainty about whether the different types of intelligence are autonomous.

Thinking scientifically → **What is 'an intelligence'?**

There is a problem of defining intelligence and there is no one single definition that would be agreed by all, or even most, psychologists. Nevertheless there is largely a consensus that traditional intellectual abilities such as verbal and numerical skills form the basis of a general intelligence that is measured by intelligence tests. However, a number of recent theories have broken with that consensus and have begun to question why some other things, such as emotional and social skills, are not regarded as part of intelligence. The theory of multiple intelligences proposed by Gardner introduced the idea that there are eight different types of intelligence. Gardner added abilities such as bodily-kinaesthetic, naturalistic and music to traditional abilities such as linguistic and logical-mathematical abilities which have been seen as the core of intelligence. Gardner sees no reason to differentiate the traditional abilities measured by intelligence tests from other abilities.

Some believe the use of the word 'intelligence' to refer to abilities such as bodily-kinaesthetic ability ignores both the traditional meaning and connotation of the word. For example, Scarr (1985) suggests that Gardner confuses talents and abilities with intelligence. This view is echoed by Sternberg (1991). Although Sternberg is an advocate of widening the concept of intelligence beyond the narrow concept of *g*, he also believes that Gardner confounds talents with intelligence. Many other researchers question whether a talent in one field represents intelligence. For example, we can recognize that a person may be a very gifted athlete but many would disagree that this necessarily indicates intelligence.

There is some confusion about the 'intelligences' that Gardner chose to include and exclude from his list. Willingham (2004) suggests that many other abilities meet the criteria that Gardner set for including them as an intelligence but have not been included. For example, Willingham believes that a humour intelligence and a memory intelligence meet Gardner's definition as both can be used to solve problems, both can be affected by brain damage, both can be shown to remarkable degree by some individuals and so on. He goes on to suggest that there are many other abilities that might be considered such as an 'olfactory intelligence'. In other words, if we were to adopt Gardner's criteria, the list of potential 'intelligences' is much greater than the eight that were eventually included in his theory.

Willingham (2004) suggests that Gardner has ignored the connotation of the word intelligence and believes this has led to confusion particularly in education. Similarly, Jensen (2009) believes that the use of the word intelligence to describe various abilities capitalizes on the high value that people place on the word 'intelligence'. He suggests the appeal of the multiple intelligences theory in education:

> has been parodied as the Marie Antoinette theory of schooling: if the people have no bread, let them eat cake. If some pupils have inordinate difficulty learning the 3 Rs, let them spend more time exercising those other skills constituting the several distinctive 'intelligences': music, art, dance, athletics, empathic understanding of other persons, or insightful understanding of oneself, and possibly a few other still debatable abilities that might intuitively qualify as 'intelligences' in Gardner's system, such as naturalist intelligence and spiritual intelligence. (p. 97)

Some believe that the appeal of theories, like Gardner's, that seek to broaden the concept of intelligence is not scientific but social and humanistic.

Information-processing approach: Anderson's theory of minimal cognitive architecture

Since the 1960s many psychologists have adopted an information-processing, or cognitive, approach to intelligence. The information-processing approach suggests that we are bombarded with information every day and that we have to select, store, retrieve and use this information in order to respond to our environment in an intelligent manner. The information-processing approach to intelligence focuses on how we use our mental capacities to process information effectively.

One such approach is Anderson's theory of minimal cognitive architecture. Anderson (1992) suggests that the psychometric tradition sees intelligence as structures identified by factor analysis. However, those like himself who are concerned with cognitive development tend to regard intelligence as something that evolves through changes in skills and knowledge. In common with Sternberg (who is discussed in the next section), he believes some of the confusion about intelligence stems from the fact that it can be studied from different perspectives. For example, research into individual differences in IQ is likely to use different concepts than research into the cognitive development of intelligence. Anderson (1999) put forward his theory of minimal cognitive architecture in an attempt to answer what he saw as central questions surrounding intelligence and development. Like Gardner, he used information from a range of sources such as traditional measures of intelligence, biological measures, neuropsychology and savants. The theory of minimal cognitive architecture is an information-processing theory.

Anderson (1992) suggests that there are low-level and high-level views of intelligence. The low-level view is a biologically based view that concentrates on measuring physiological processes. The high-level view is concerned with higher order skills such as reasoning which are cognitive-level explanations. He suggests that any theory of intelligence needs to explain both views. He has identified two clusters of questions related to these views: one concerned with regularities in the data; and the other with exceptions to those regularities. These questions form a series of agenda items that any theory would minimally need to address (Anderson, 1999).

The regularities are:

1 'Cognitive abilities increase with development' (Anderson, 1999, p. 10). Abilities associated with fluid intelligence tend to increase during adolescence and abilities associated with crystallized intelligence tend to increase into middle age (Gardner, Kornhaber and Wake, 1996).
2 'Individual differences in intelligence are stable with development' (Anderson, 1999, p. 10). Individuals' IQ levels remain constant relative to others.
3 'Cognitive abilities co-vary' (Anderson, 1999, p. 10). Individuals who do well on one psychometric test tend to do well on others whereas those that do poorly on one do poorly on others.

Anderson (1999) argues that these regularities can be explained by low-level, biologically based theories. This type of theory would explain the regularities in terms of neural functioning.

The major exceptions are:

4 Some individuals who have normal or above average intelligence have specific problems or deficits in cognitive functioning. For example, individuals who show intelligence in all other spheres may have problems with spelling.
5 Some individuals who have a below average intelligence have specific skills which show high levels of cognitive functioning. For example, savants may have problems with general intelligence but are gifted in music or use of number.
6 Some cognitive mechanisms seem to be universal and show no individual differences. These mechanisms are shown in individuals

that show very low intelligence in other spheres. Examples of such mechanisms include language acquisition and seeing in three dimensions, both of which are more computationally complex than many other 'everyday' cognitive abilities (Anderson, 1999).

Anderson (1999) argues that a low-level biological view cannot explain both the regularities and the exceptions. He suggests the only way to explain both is to use a higher level of explanation; a cognitive-level or information-processing explanation.

Theory of minimum cognitive architecture

Anderson (1999) points out that intelligence tests measure intelligence by assessing knowledge. He suggests that knowledge is acquired via two very different routes. These different routes do not have the same relationship to IQ differences and developmental change.

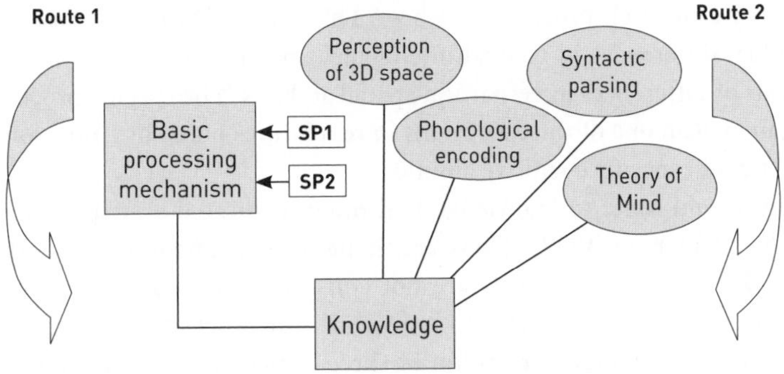

Figure 6.3 Anderson's theory of minimal cognitive architecture

The first route to acquiring knowledge is through thinking. In the theory, thought is constrained by the speed of the basic processing mechanism (BPM). The hypothesis is that speed of processing is unchanged with development and is an innate component of individual differences. It is this that underlies the general intelligence, *g*. Anderson believes a general intelligence is shown in the correlations found among psychometric tests. Anderson (1992, p. 58) claims that *g* stems from 'low-level cognitive processes that underlie intelligent thinking'. The psychometric tests show variations among individuals because these basic processes vary in speed between people. Since knowledge is acquired through thinking, fast processing facilitates acquisition and slow processing hinders it.

In addition to the BPM, Anderson proposes there are also two specific processors. One specific processor is for verbal representations, the other for spatial. Both processors are implemented by the BPM. The concept of specific processors is based on evidence from psychometric tests and neuropsychology (Gardner, Kornhaber and Wake, 1996). Some psychometric theories suggest group factors of verbal and spatial abilities. Neuropsychological evidence shows hemispheric differences with left hemisphere governing language and mathematical abilities, and the right governing spatial functions. Anderson suggests that each specific processor has a latent power or potential. The latent power of each specific processor is unrelated to the other. However, the performance of each processor is a result of the latent power and the speed of the BPM. If the BPM speed is slow, the specific processors will be limited, no matter what the latent power. However, if the BPM speed is fast, it allows the latent power of each processor to show. Thus, the BPM is the cause of individual differences in general intelligence and specific processors are the basis of differences in verbal and spatial abilities. The specific processors can explain one of the exceptions in regularities noted by Anderson: differences in specific cognitive abilities.

The second route to knowledge is through dedicated systems called modules (Anderson, 1999). These are thought to operate independently of the BPM and consequently are not constrained by its speed. They therefore show no relationship to individual differences in intelligence. These modules include perception of three-dimensional space, phonological encoding, theory of mind and so on. In addition to being independent of the BPM, Anderson proposes that each module also functions independently of the others. Although separate from the BPM, Gardner, Kornhaber and Wake, (1996, p. 218) point out that the modules perform 'complex computations of evolutionary significance'. Whereas the acquisition of knowledge via route 1 varies because of differences in BPM speed, the acquisition of knowledge via the modules does not vary. Anderson uses the example of a person with Down syndrome who may have problems with simple arithmetic yet can recognize that another person holds beliefs and that these will guide their actions. The person's knowledge of arithmetic is acquired via the BPM but the knowledge of others is acquired via the independent theory of mind module. Modules therefore explain another of the exceptions to the regularities: there are universal cognitive mechanisms that do not show individual differences. Evidence for modules comes from studies of brain-damaged people. For example, various visual agnosias affect perception and recognition but not intelligence. The selective impairment shown in these cases indicates some damage to particular modules. In contrast, savants may have damaged BPM but functioning and effective modules, since savants do very poorly on traditional measures of intelligence but are talented in one specific ability. The notion of modules may also explain why cognitive abilities increase with age. The increase may be linked to the maturation of modules. This maturation may underlie the rapid qualitative changes seen in childhood (Gardner, Kornhaber and Wake, 1996). For example, the maturation of a language module would allow a child to use linguistic abilities in acquiring and storing knowledge via the BPM. This would result in a qualitative change in knowledge acquisition.

Although the theory of minimal cognitive architecture seems to be an elegant way of combining psychometric and developmental views, there are some reservations about it. The theory focuses solely on information processing and does not consider other factors such as the role of culture (Gardner, Kornhaber and Wake, 1996). Some claim that elements of the theory lack evidence (Deary, 1992). Finally, the notion that modules show no individual differences has been questioned.

Summary

Anderson identified two clusters of items that a theory of intelligence should address. The first were a group of regularities in intelligence that could be explained by low-level biologically based theories and explanation. The second were exceptions to the regularities. The regularities and exceptions could only be explained by a high-level cognitive explanation of intelligence. The theory of minimum cognitive architecture suggests there are two routes to acquiring knowledge needed for intelligence. The first is through thinking. Thought is constrained by the speed of a basic processing mechanism (BPM). Differences in the speed of the BPM are the source of differences in general intelligence. Two specific processors, one visual and one spatial, run via the BPM. Although both these specific processors have their own latent power, the expression of this power is constrained by the speed of the BPM. The theory also postulates the existence of modules that are independent of the BPM. Since they are independent, they are not related to the speed of the BPM and, therefore, general intelligence.

Information-processing approach: Sternberg's triarchic theory of intelligence

Sternberg (1985) believes that many theories of intelligence are not wrong but merely incomplete. He suggests that the general factor, *g*, is an artefact of the limited populations of individuals tested, the materials used in the tests and the methods used in the tests (Sternberg, 2002). He believes it is time to expand the notion of what it means to be intelligent or, as he puts it, 'to move beyond conventional theories of intelligence' (2002, p. 73). Thus, he has proposed a triarchic theory that tries to encompass all aspects of intelligence. The triarchic theory is composed of three interrelated parts or subtheories: componential, experiential and contextual. Each subtheory refers to a different aspect of intelligence. The componential subtheory refers to the mental mechanisms or the information processes that underlie intelligent behaviour. The experiential subtheory deals with both external and internal aspects of intelligence (that is, it explores how experience affects intelligence and how intelligence affects experience). The contextual subtheory considers intelligence in relation to the context of culture and environment that the individual is in.

The componential subtheory

The componential subtheory is concerned with the internal aspects of intelligence. In other words, it considers what mental processes are at work during intelligent activity. It is the analytical component of intelligence. Gardner, Kornhaber and Wake (1996) suggest it is the most highly elaborated subtheory because it is based on Sternberg's research into information processing. Sternberg (2002) hypothesizes that the information-processing components underlying successful intelligence are universal. Thus, although the solutions chosen for a problem may vary across cultures and environments, the need to define the problem and translate this into a strategy exists in all cultures. Sternberg describes three kinds of components that are used in intelligent activity:

- *Metacomponents* are the mental mechanisms used to supervise intelligent activity. They are used to recognize a problem and develop strategy to solve it. They then monitor the strategy and evaluate it.

- *Performance components* carry out the tasks identified by the metacomponents. They are the processes involved in solving a problem.
- *Knowledge-acquisition components* include the processes involved in acquiring new information. These processes include selective combination, which enables the adding of new information, selective encoding, which allows relevant and irrelevant information to be filtered, and selective comparison, which allows new information to be compared to old.

The metacomponents are described as higher-level processes while the performance and knowledge-acquisition components are described as lower-level processes. The metacomponent acts as a sort of executive that activates and directs the other two components. Sternberg uses an example of a person writing a research paper (or essay) to illustrate how the three parts interact. The metacomponents are used when the person decides what to write about, organizes the work, monitors the writing and evaluates the finished work. The knowledge-acquisition components would enable the person to search for the right material and combine the information to fit into the work. The performance components are used in the writing of the work by searching the correct words or examples from memory.

The experiential subtheory

The experiential subtheory looks at how experience is linked to intelligence. This subtheory is the creative component of intelligence. Sternberg suggests that a given problem does not need the same level of use of the information-processing components for different people. A person with experience of the problem requires less use of mental resources than a person with less experience. For example, each year I ask my students to try to solve a complex problem (the 'hobbit and orc problem'). Students who have never encountered the problem before find this very difficult and almost impossible to solve. However, those who have come across it find it hard but solvable. I use it every year and, although I have not memorized the solution, I arrive at the solution very quickly. This is not due to differences in internal intelligence but to a difference in our experiences of the problem.

Sternberg points out that experience of a task or problem falls on a continuum from being completely new or novel to being automated. Thus the experiential subtheory suggests that intelligence is the function of two abilities: the ability to do new tasks (or novelty); and the ability to learn to such a degree that solution becomes automatic (or automization).

The contextual subtheory

The contextual subtheory is about the external aspects of intelligence and is concerned with the application of componential intelligence to the real world. This subtheory is therefore the practical component of intelligence. Sternberg suggests that internal intelligence, the componential subtheory, is constantly interacting with external. We need processes to be able to show intelligence into the environmental context. Sternberg proposes that there are three types of mental process that are central to the contextual subtheory: adaptation, selection and shaping.

- Adaptation is the process of adapting behaviour to the environment the individual finds themself in. For example, a college student might need to adapt between the different demands of college in the week and the different demands of working in a shop at weekends.
- Selection involves selecting one of several different environments. For example, if someone has a choice of jobs, one involving verbal skills and the other mental arithmetic, they might choose the environment that best fits their skills.
- Shaping involves trying to alter the environment to achieve a better fit (that is, instead of the individual trying to adapt to the environment they try to adapt the environment to them).

According to Sternberg an individual will first try to adapt to the environment. If this is not possible then they will use one of the other two processes.

The contextual subtheory is not measured well by traditional IQ tests. Sternberg suggested it was best measured using a concept he called tacit knowledge.

Tacit knowledge is based on procedures rather than facts and is the knowledge about how to do something. Sternberg et al. (1995) define tacit knowledge as action-oriented knowledge. Measures of tacit knowledge tend to be used in applied settings since they are largely domain specific (that is, they apply to one type of environment). For example, the tacit knowledge used by a mechanical engineer will be different to that of an electrician.

Overview of the triarchic theory

Sternberg's theory is very ambitious as he tries to encompass all aspects of intelligence. Gardner, Kornhaber and Wake (1996) believe that the greatest strength of the theory is that it brings together diverse elements of intelligence. It tries to show how internal mental mechanisms are used to fit intelligently into the external world. Sternberg (2002) is interested in how people function in the real world. He claims the theory is successful and shows construct validations regardless of the environment where testing takes place (that is, laboratory, schools or workplace). Like Gardner, Sternberg's theory has been influential in education since it identifies the information-processing skills used in intellectual activities. For example, Sternberg (1997) describes a five-year project that 'infused' his triarchic theory into the instruction and assessment of high-school students. Students were identified as being strong in one of analytic, creative or practical abilities. They were then taught one course in a way that emphasized their respective abilities. This improved their performance on the course.

However, Gardner, Kornhaber and Wake (1996) claim the comprehensive nature of the triarchic theory leads to a weakness. They suggest that, because it encompasses so much, it is not coherent. Unlike Gardner's and Anderson's theories, Sternberg does not provide an explanation of why individuals can be either gifted or impaired in a particular intellectual ability. Another criticism of the theory is that it tends to ignore biological aspects of intelligence (Gardner, Kornhaber and Wake, 1996). None of the components or processes mention in the theory are linked to brain functioning.

Summary

The triarchic theory of intelligence is composed of three interrelated parts or subtheories: componential, experiential and contextual. The componential subtheory is concerned with the internal aspects of intelligence and has three sets of components; metacomponents, performance components and knowledge-acquisition components. The experiential subtheory looks at how experience is linked to intelligence. A person's experience of a task or problem falls on a continuum from being completely new or novel to being automated. The contextual subtheory is about external aspects of intelligence and is concerned with the application of the componential intelligence to real world. Three mental processes are used for this, adaptation, shaping and selection. This subtheory is best measured by assessing tacit knowledge. The great strength of the theory is that it brings together many diverse elements of intelligence.

Emotional intelligence

The focus of most of the theories of intelligence discussed so far has been on rational thought and reasoning. None of the theories, with the exception of Gardner's multiple intelligences theory, tackled the more emotional (affective) elements of intelligence. This was addressed by the concept of **emotional intelligence** that was first proposed by Salovey and Mayer (1990). In a broad sense, it is to do with knowledge of how emotions work and having the ability to use this knowledge. It is defined as:

> the ability to perceive and express emotion accurately and adaptively, the ability to understand emotion and emotional knowledge, the ability to use feelings to facilitate thought, and the ability to regulate emotions in oneself and others. **(Salovey and Pizarro, 2002, p. 263)**

The concept of emotional intelligence was popularized by Goleman (1995) and gained much attention from the media. Consequently, as Salovey and Pizarro (2002) point out, like other ideas that capture public interest, the term has become diffuse and imprecise, making it difficult to evaluate. The idea of 'improving' emotional intelligence was seen as a way of curing society's ills. The concept became linked to moral character, conscientiousness, self-control and so on (Salovey and Pizarro, 2002). Few of the popular claims made about emotional intelligence had any empirical support. As a result, Eysenck (2004) suggests that the broad and vague definition adopted by Goleman is of little use in a scientific context. This section will concentrate on the scientific rather than the popular meaning of the term.

Salovey and Pizarro (2002) argue that the scientific concept of emotional intelligence is useful for two reasons: firstly, the idea of emotional intelligence provides an organizing framework to synthesize the work on affective phenomena; and secondly, it goes beyond traditional views of intelligence to incorporate emotional competences.

Mayer and Salovey (1997) describe emotional intelligence as having four branches: perceiving emotions, using emotions to facilitate thought, understanding emotions, and managing emotions.

- The 'perceiving emotions' branch is concerned with the ability to perceive emotions both in the individual and in others. This involves attending to emotional expressions and behaviour and appraising this accurately. Salovey and Pizarro (2002) suggest that it also includes the ability to perceive emotion in art such as literature or music.
- The 'using emotions to facilitate thought' branch focuses on how emotion affects the cognitive system. It includes the ability to include emotion in reasoning and problem solving. Salovey and Pizarro (2002) describe this branch as the harnessing of emotions to make decision-making and creative activities more effective. They point out that, although emotions can disrupt cognition, they can also help to focus on what is important and foster creative thinking (for example in creating art).
- The 'understanding emotions' branch is based on the idea that emotions are a complex part of human experience that almost requires its own language. One of the skills included in this branch is the ability to label emotions accurately. Another is the ability to understand the antecedents of emotion. Salovey and Pizarro (2002) believe this is a critical component of emotional intelligence. We can only learn to deal with emotions in ourselves and others if we can understand how the emotions begin and develop. Understanding emotions is vital in our transactions with others.
- The 'managing emotions' branch is concerned with the ability to regulate emotions in oneself and in others. It includes the ability to work with feelings rather than repressing them. This may also include being open to feelings.

Mayer, Caruso and Salovey (1999) developed the Multi-Factor Emotional Intelligence Scale (MEIS) to measure these four branches of emotional intelligence. This scale was a great improvement on previous measures, which Davies, Stankov and Roberts (1998) suggest were unreliable and related to various personality dimensions. Nevertheless, Salovey and Pizarro (2002) point out that there were some problems with the MEIS scale. For example, it took a long time to administer and contained some items that needed improvement. Mayer, Salovey and Caruso (2002) have developed a successor to the MEIS called the Mayer-Salovey-Caruso Emotional Intelligence Test (MSCEIT). This is also based on the four-branch model of emotional intelligence put forward by Mayer and Salovey (1997) and has two subtasks for each branch. This test shows good **internal reliability** and seems to show discriminant validity from traditional intelligence and personality tests (Salovey and Pizarro, 2002). After further studies Mayer, Salovey and Caruso (2004, p. 211) concluded that the MSCEIT is 'highly reliable at the total-score, area, and branch levels, and provides a reasonably valid measure of EI'. Palmer, Gignac, Manocha and Stough (2005) agree that the total and branch levels are reliable but suggest that the subscale reliability was low. However, a study of the MSCEIT using 111 Norwegian executives showed poor reliability on all scales (Follesdal and Hagtvet, 2009).

Salovey and Pizarro (2002) believe the concept of emotional intelligence has been useful as a mechanism for conveying the idea of an important but neglected set of competences. It has also been useful for organizing the literature on emotional intelligence and to help in the study of relationships between emotion and reason. Researchers have also used theories about emotional intelligence to develop psychometric scales to study the concept. However, there remains a doubt about whether these measure something different to existing scales. Roberts, Zeidner and Matthews (2001, p. 200) conclude 'it remains unclear whether there is anything about EI that psychologists working within the fields of personality, intelligence, and applied psychological research do not already know'.

Bar-On model of emotional-social intelligence

Bar-On (2006) put forward an alternative model of intelligence that incorporates both emotional and social skills. Bar-On adopts an evolutionary psychological perspective to emotional and social intelligence. He points out that Darwin's work highlighted the importance of emotional expression for survival. In his theory, Bar-On emphasizes the importance of both emotional and social skills for successful adaptation to living in social groups. In addition, the theory also draws on the concepts of intrapersonal and interpersonal intelligence introduced by Gardner (1983). Like Gardner, Bar-On, Tranel, Denburg and Bechara (2003) link the various features in his theory to brain mechanisms.

The Bar-On model suggests that emotional-social intelligence is:

> a cross-section of interrelated emotional and social competencies, skills and facilitators that determine how well we understand and express ourselves, understand others and relate with them, and cope with daily demands, challenges and pressures. (http://www.reuven-baron.org/bar-on-model/essay.php?i=2 accessed 18/4/2010)

The emotional and social competences include five meta-factors. The meta-factors are:

1. Intrapersonal (self-awareness and self-expression)
2. Interpersonal (social awareness and interaction)
3. Stress Management (emotional management and control)
4. Adaptability (change management)
5. General Mood (self-motivation)

In addition, Bar-On identified 15 interrelated skills that make up the meta-factors. They are:

- Intrapersonal – self-regard, emotional self-awareness, assertiveness, independence, self-actualization
- Interpersonal – empathy, social responsibility, interpersonal relationships
- Stress management – stress tolerance, impulse control
- Adaptability – reality testing, flexibility, problem solving
- General mood – optimism, happiness

Bar-On has developed a number of scales to measure emotional-social intelligence including the BarOn Emotional Quotient Inventory (EQ-i). The scale is not designed to measure traditional cognitive abilities but to assess the five meta-factors and the ability to deal with demands and pressures. Bar-On claims the scale is a reliable and valid measure of emotional intelligence (Bar-On, 2004; Bar-On, Brown, Kirkcaldy and Thome, 2000). However others have expressed doubts about the validity of self-reports in this area (for example Kluemper, 2008).

Summary

Salovey and Mayer (1990) first proposed the concept of emotional intelligence. They suggest it is concerned with knowledge of how emotions work and the ability to use this knowledge. Mayer and Salovey (1997) describe emotional intelligence as having four branches: perceiving emotions, using emotions to facilitate thought, understanding emotions, and managing emotions. These four branches are measured by the Mayer-Salovey-Caruso Emotional Intelligence Test (MSCEIT). Studies of the MSCEIT suggest it is a reliable and valid psychometric measure of emotional intelligence. The Bar-On model of emotional-social intelligence comprises five meta-factors: intrapersonal, interpersonal, stress management, adaptability, general mood. These are measured using the EQ-i but doubts have been raised about the validity of the scale.

Further reading

Gardner, H. (2006) *Multiple Intelligences: New Horizons.* New York: Basic Books.

Gardner, H., Kornhaber, M.L. and Wake, W.K. (1996) *Intelligence: Multiple Perspectives.* Fort Worth, TX: Harcourt Brace College.

Sternberg, R.J. and Grigorenko, E.L. (eds) (2002) *The General Factor of Intelligence: How General Is It?* Mahwah, NJ: Lawrence Erlbaum Associates.

Sternberg, R.J., Lautrey, J. and Lubard, T.I. (eds) (2002) *Models of Intelligence: International Perspectives.* Washington, DC: American Psychological Society.

Chapter 7

Intelligence test performance

People vary in the abilities they have. Some people have good verbal skills; others are good at visual art; while others may have good mechanical skills. Some of these differences are reflected in levels of intelligence. Differences in intelligence are measured using these types of psychometric tests. These tests are used to give a standard measure of intelligence, IQ. Intelligence tests are used to assess variations in intelligence (as shown by IQ scores) in the population. There has been a long, and at times heated, debate among psychologists about the source of this variation. One potential source of the variation is genetic. It may be that variations in human intelligence are genetically determined and have relatively little to do with upbringing. The other potential source of the variation is environmental. There are many environmental factors that might affect intelligence such as the family, level of stimulation, schooling or even culture. One reason the debate between the genetic and environmental camps is so heated is that it has political and social consequences. It has long been recognized that genetics and environment interact, therefore the debate centres on the relative contribution of each.

This chapter will cover:

- Intelligence testing
- Genetic influence on intelligence
- Environmental influences on intelligence
- Culture and intelligence
- Interaction of genetics and environment

Intelligence testing

Intelligence can be measured in a number of ways. For example, one might use physiological measures such as reaction time, cognitive measures such as the Cognitive Assessment System (Naglieri and Das, 1997), or psychometric tests such as the ones mentioned in the last chapter (for example Binet-Simon tests, Wechsler Intelligence Scale for Children and Wechsler Adult Intelligence Scale).

The focus of this chapter is on psychometric measures of intelligence. Modern psychometric tests are designed to measure many different aspects of intelligence, including vocabulary, comprehension, spatial ability and so on. These various factors are measured using subscales. The tests are 'standardized tests'. Standardized tests are given to a large sample of the population they are designed for (for example to children of particular age, to adults over 16 and so on). Neisser et al. (1996) point out that, for historical reasons, the scores from these intelligence tests are referred to as IQ scores. The tests are used to give measure of IQ, which is an overall score that reflects all the subscales. IQ is therefore best seen as a measure of general intelligence or *g*. The scores of the large sample are used to give a normal distribution of scores. By convention, the mean score of the sample is given a value of 100 and standard deviations from the sample are used to calculate scores above and below the mean. Also by convention, one standard deviation is 15 points. This means that the IQ of approximately 95 per cent of the population falls between 70 and 130 (or two standard deviations from the mean). Any individual taking a standardized test can be allocated an IQ score by noting where their score falls in the established distribution of scores for their population. Like any good psychometric test, intelligence tests should be reliable and valid.

Reliability of tests

Reliability is concerned with the consistency of test scores. Psychometric tests assume that psychological variables such as intelligence remain relatively stable over time. If an intelligence score is low on one occasion and high on another over a short time interval then the test is not reliable. This type of reliability, **external reliability**, can be assessed using the test-retest method. This involves testing a number of participants on two separate occasions. The two sets of scores are then correlated. A high positive correlation indicates that the test is reliable but a low correlation shows poor reliability.

However, in practice, intelligence as measured by IQ tests fluctuates from one occasion to another. This can be by as much as 15 points (Benson, 2003), which is equivalent to one standard deviation on standardized tests. There are a number of possible reasons for this. Firstly, individual performance can vary. People can have 'good days' and 'bad days' due to a variety of factors such as sleep, mood, illness and so on. Secondly, the tests may show practice effects as, if someone has taken the test once, it will influence their performance on subsequent tests. The person may have learned some of the answers or developed a better understanding of some of the techniques used in the test.

Another part of reliability is **internal reliability.** This is concerned with the internal consistency of a test. Tests typically have a number of different elements or subscales in them. If these correlate positively with each other then this indicates good internal reliability. Researchers also examine the individual items in each subscale and again there should be a positive correlation if the test has internal reliability. If it does not, then it is often seen as a reason to omit individual items. Modern psychometric tests of intelligence have good internal validity.

Validity of tests

The **validity** of any test is concerned with whether the test actually measures what it claims to measure. A valid test of intelligence should be measuring intelligence and not some other variable. To show validity, a test should first show reliability (if the test is a true measure of a stable construct then it should give the same scores each time). Validity is more difficult to assess than reliability and there are various types to consider. **Face validity** is the simplest form and is concerned with whether the test seems to be measuring intelligence or a factor of intelligence. **Concurrent validity** involves the comparison of the test results with some other measure of intelligence. If the two measures are well correlated this would be evidence of concurrent validity. An intelligence test shows **predictive validity** if it can be shown to predict future performance in something that requires intelligence. For example, if IQ scores in childhood showed a strong correlation with GCSE grades then the test would have predictive validity. Although there are other forms of validity (such as construct and discriminative), most research has concentrated on the concurrent and predictive validity of intelligence.

Many studies of validity have focused on whether IQ scores predict future school performance, occupational status, income and so on. In a review of the area, Mackintosh (1998) reports that there are positive correlations between IQ and most of the variables studied. However, some variables are better correlated than others. For example, there is a better correlation between IQ and academic success than between IQ and future income. In another review, Neisser et al. (1996, p. 81) report that intelligence tests 'do in fact predict school performance fairly well' and point out that the relationship between IQ scores and learning at school has been found wherever it has been studied. They note (p. 82) 'There may be styles of teaching and methods of instruction that will decrease or increase this correlation, but none that consistently eliminates it has yet been found'. Neisser et al. (1996) also report that scores on intelligence tests predict job performance as measured by supervisor ratings or work samples. However, they note that correlations in this area are moderate and that other characteristics such as personality were probably of equal importance. Scores of intelligence tests are negatively correlated with other types of outcome. For example, IQ scores are negatively correlated with levels of juvenile crime.

IQ and intelligence

Although intelligence tests may be generally reliable and show some validity, there are still some problems with them as a measure of intelligence. One problem is that, while intelligence tests might be measuring part of a person's intelligence, they do not measure *all* of a person's intelligence. Intelligence tests might be a good measure of *g* but not everyone agrees that *g* exists (or if it does, it is not the sole aspect of intelligence). Gardner and Sternberg have very different conceptions of intelligence to the traditional psychometric view, much of which is not measured by traditional tests of IQ. Both Gardner and Sternberg have attempted to construct tests that reflect a broader view of intelligence. For example, Sternberg and Rainbow Project Collaborators (2006) have devised a different type of test that is broader than traditional tests of intelligence. Like traditional tests, the test measures analytical skills but it also assesses creative and practical skills. Sternberg et al. (2006) claimed that the Rainbow measures showed good predictive validity and reduced ethnic group differences. They suggest these measures could increase diversity and equity in admissions to colleges. Traditional tests have focused on reasoning and analytical skills while ignoring others such as interpersonal skills or emotional skills. Mayer, Salovey and Caruso (2002) have redressed the balance by developing the Mayer-Salovey-Caruso Emotional Intelligence Test (MSCEIT) to measure emotional intelligence.

Howe (1997) suggests the main problem with intelligence tests is more fundamental: a lack of an operational definition for intelligence. Psychologists do not agree what is meant by the term intelligence. If there is no agreement about the concept you are trying to measure, how can it be measured? Howe illustrates the problem with another psychological construct: vanity. Like intelligence, vanity has no clear-cut definition. Any psychologist who was developing a psychometric scale to measure vanity would have to use questions that they assumed measured it. If the answers to the questions correspond to others' judgement about vanity, the test maker may claim they have a valid 'measure' of vanity. However, Howe points out it is not a *real* measure of vanity, only one that corresponds to some psychologist's *opinion* of what vanity is. Others may, and probably would, have different views and would develop very different tests. Howe concludes that this is the position we have in the measurement of intelligence and claims (p. 6) 'nothing is genuinely being measured'.

Summary

Most intelligence testing uses psychometric measures of intelligence. The tests are used to give measures of IQ, which by convention have a mean score of 100. To be useful, intelligence tests should be reliable and valid. Reliability is concerned with the consistency of test scores. There are two types of reliability: external and internal. External reliability can be assessed using the test-retest method. Internal reliability is concerned with the internal consistency of a test. The validity of any test is concerned with whether the test actually measures what it claims to measure. There are many types of validity but the two usually used in the assessment of intelligence tests are predictive and concurrent validity. Studies of intelligence test validity suggest that they are reasonably good predictors of some variables such as school performance. However, there are two major problems with intelligence tests. The first is that the tests do not measure all of intelligence. The second is that, since there is no agreed definition of intelligence, it is not possible to be sure the tests measure it at all.

Genetic influence on intelligence

One potential source of the variation in intelligence scores between people is genetic. Before examining the evidence for a genetic influence on intelligence, there are a number of things to consider. Firstly, there is nearly complete agreement that any variation in intelligence is due to both genetic and environmental factors (Sternberg and Grigorenko, 1997). Secondly, genes interact with environmental factors to produce intelligence; they are interdependent (Plomin, 1990). The genes we inherit give us a genetic potential, or genotype. The way this potential is shown (or the phenotype) depends on how the genes interact with environmental factors. Lastly, although psychologists could in theory manipulate environments to isolate the relative effects of genetics and environment, in reality they cannot because of both ethical and practical considerations. Therefore many of the studies of the genetic influence on intelligence are correlational or natural experiments. There are three main ways of studying whether there is a genetic influence on intelligence: family studies, twin studies, and adoption studies.

Family studies

Family studies examine similarities among family members. The argument is that, if variation in intelligence is genetic, the greater the genetic similarity the more similar intelligence (or IQ) should be. This can be shown by examining the strength of correlations in IQ between family members. In general it is found that genetically closer relatives have higher correlations of IQ. For example, in a meta-analysis Bouchard and McGue (1981) found the average correlation for identical twins (100 per cent genetic similarity) was +0.86 but for siblings (50 per cent genetic similarity) it was +0.47. Cousins, who only share 25 per cent of their genes, showed a correlation of +0.15. The correlation for unrelated people is 0.

This seems to support the idea that genetics plays a part in intelligence score variation. However, the effect of genetics is not clear because of other confounding variables. Those people with the greater genetic similarity typically have greater environmental similarity. Identical twins grow up together, siblings do not grow up at the same time but they are raised by the same family. Cousins, however, typically live apart.

Twin studies

One of the most useful ways of studying the influence of genetics is to use a special type of family study, the study of different types of twin. There are two types of twin, identical and fraternal. Identical twins develop from the same fertilized ovum or zygote and are therefore more correctly called monozygotic twins (MZ). Since they develop from one zygote, they essentially have the same genes. Fraternal twins develop from two zygotes and are therefore called dizygotic (DZ). DZ twins are no more alike than other siblings and share 50 per cent of their genes.

In one type of twin study, the correlations of intelligence scores for sets of MZ twins are compared to the correlations found in DZ twins. The rationale behind these studies is that both sets of twins share very similar environments (being raised at the same time in the same household) but MZ twins share more genes than DZ twins. If genetics plays a major part in variation of intelligence scores then there should be a higher correlation of scores in MZ than DZ twins. However, if environment plays a major part then there should be no difference (since both sets of twins share the same environment). Bouchard and McGue (1981) collated the evidence from 111 studies of intelligence and twins and found that the mean correlation for intelligence in MZ twins is +0.86 and is +0.60 for DZ twins. This fact, that the intelligence scores of MZ twins are more similar than DZ, suggests that a genetic factor plays a major role. However, there are a number of flaws in simply comparing MZ and DZ twins. One of the main ones is that since MZ twins look the same they are treated more alike than DZ twins (Loehlin and Nichols, 1976). DZ twins do not necessarily look alike and can be different genders. They are more likely to be treated differently. Thus the greater similarity in IQ scores found in MZ twins may reflect greater environmental similarity rather than genetic similarity.

Another type of twin study tries to overcome this problem by studying MZ twins who have been reared apart and comparing them to twins who have been reared together. The MZ twins reared apart share identical genes but different environments. Shields (1962) found that there was very little difference in the correlations of intelligence scores between MZ twins reared together and apart (+0.77 and +0.76 respectively). The correlation for DZ twins was only +0.51. This seems to be stronger evidence of a genetic influence on intelligence since the MZ twins reared apart did not share environments. In a meta-analysis, Ridley (1999) found similar average figures: +0.86 for MZ twins reared together, +0.76 for MZ twins reared apart and +0.51 for DZ twins reared together. Since the MZ twins reared apart had higher correlations of intelligence scores than the DZ twins reared together, this provides support for the idea of a strong genetic component in the variation in intelligence scores.

In a review of twin studies Bouchard (1997) concludes that the only explanation for the similarities in IQ of MZ twins reared apart is that there is a genetic influence. Bouchard suggests these findings are consistent with other studies of behaviour-genetics such as adult kinships. Nevertheless there are problems with these studies. In many cases the MZ twins reared 'apart' were actually brought up by different people in the same family and were in close contact. These twins shared both genes and environment.

Thinking scientifically → **Validity of twin studies**

Twin studies are a popular method for assessing the relative contribution of genetic and environmental factors in human traits and abilities. Twin studies have been described as a superb natural experiment (Martin, Boomsma and Machin, 1997). The assumption is that the key difference between MZ and DZ twins is the degree of genetic similarity. Therefore if the degree of similarity between MZ twins is greater than that between DZ twins it demonstrates a genetic influence.

However, not everyone shares these assumptions and there are a number of problems with twin studies. One of these problems is the study of twins becomes effectively a natural experiment where there is no random selection of participants (since twins are relatively rare) and no random selection into one group or another. A potentially more serious problem is a lack of population validity (Howe, 1997). There are many aspects of being a twin that make the applicability of evidence from them to the rest of the population doubtful. Howe suggests that the lives of twins, particularly MZ twins, are different from other, non-twin people. Evans and Martin (2000) point out that twins differ from singletons in several important ways. For example, twins tend to have lower birth weights and more complications during birth. Twins have a lower average IQ score compared to singletons particularly on verbal reasoning scales (Record, McKeown and Edwards, 1970).

Another problem with twin studies is the assumption that the only difference between MZ and DZ twins is the degree of genetic similarity. Many researchers have pointed out that the evidence shows that

MZ twins are treated more alike by parents and peers and are more likely to have the same friends (Kamin and Goldberger, 2002). Howe (1997) notes that in many studies of twins 'reared apart', the separated twins were not fully separated but continued to have regular contact. In many cases the twins were raised by different parts of the same family group. Howe reports that the correlation coefficient of IQ for MZ twins reared in same family was 0.83 but was only 0.47 when the twins were raised by completely different families. The underestimation of the role of the environment may result in an overestimate of the role of genetics.

Adoption studies

Another method of assessing the contribution of genetics and environment is to use adoption studies. This method involves comparing the intelligence of adopted children to both adoptive and biological parents. If environment plays a major role in intelligence variability then the child should be more similar to adoptive parent. However, if genetics plays a major role then the child should be more similar to biological parent. Most studies find a greater similarity to the biological parent then the adoptive parent (for example Mackintosh, 1998) thus suggesting that the role of genetics is greater than the role of the environment. In a study of IQ in a Texas adoption project, Loehlin, Horn and Willerman (1997) found a major contribution to IQ variability is genetic. They found that shared family environment has an effect on IQ, but only when the children are young. In contrast, the genetic effects increased with age and by the time the children were in late adolescence the effect of shared environment was minor compared to a genetic factor.

One problem in the interpretation of adoption studies is the policy of selective placement used by some adoption agencies. This is the policy of placing children into backgrounds similar to those they came from. Therefore some of the similarity between children and their biological parent may be due to environmental similarity.

Conclusions

The evidence from the family, twin and adoption studies all suggest that the variation in intelligence scores has a strong genetic component. However, there are a number of issues to be considered. The evidence is not about the *total* levels of intelligence but the just contribution of genetic and environmental factors to the variation in intelligence score. There is a distinction between heritability and genetic determination. The evidence discussed here is about heritability; it does not suggest that some aspects of intelligence are genetically determined. Heritability is the proportion of the variation in intelligence that is associated with genetic factors. As Neisser et al. (1996) point out, heritability does not imply immutability. Eysenck (2004) illustrates the difference between heritability and genetic determination using the example of the number of fingers people have. This is almost entirely determined by genetic factors. Heritability is concerned only with the factors that cause some people to have more or fewer fingers. Mackintosh (1998) claims that it is not possible to estimate the heritability of IQ in modern societies with any precision and suggests it is anywhere between 30 per cent and 75 per cent.

There are also other issues to be considered. Apart from the problem of estimating heritability accurately, any estimates are only relevant for the population being studied. Heritability varies from one population to another and estimates gathered from one group of people or one culture cannot be applied to another (Brace, 1996). So, for example, heritability estimates from a white middle-class population cannot be applied to other groups. Finally, Wahlsten and Gottlieb (1997) criticize some of the work in behaviour genetics and suggest that explanations for IQ differences need to be considered at a range of levels (such as culture, society, immediate environment, physiology, genes). They suggest it is very difficult to reach conclusions until all levels are considered.

Summary

There may be a genetic influence on the variation in IQ but it is difficult to separate from environmental influences. There are three ways of studying genetic influence on intelligence: family studies, twin studies and adoption studies. Family studies show a higher correlation of IQ between family members who have greater genetic similarity (for example siblings show higher correlations than cousins). However, this may also be due to greater environmental similarity rather than genetic similarity. Comparisons of correlations between different types of twins show that MZ twins have a higher correlation than DZ twins. However, this could be influenced by environmental factors, MZ twins are treated more alike. Studies of MZ twins reared apart show they demonstrate a higher correlation of IQ than DZ twins reared together. This seems to be very strong evidence for a genetic influence on IQ variation. Adoption studies show a greater correlation between children and their biological parent than between children and their adoptive parent. This is further evidence of a genetic influence on IQ. It is difficult to estimate the influence of genetic factors in the variation of IQ but estimates of heritability suggest it is between 30 and 75 per cent.

Environmental influences on intelligence

The American Psychological Association (APA) task force studying intelligence identified a number of environmental influences on intelligence. Two sets of environmental influences were grouped into biological and social variables. The biological variables from the environment include nutrition, lead, alcohol and prenatal factors. The social variables include occupation, schooling, interventions and family environment. This section will consider some of the biological and social variables. Other factors such as the Flynn effect and culture will be considered in separate sections.

Biological variables

There are a number of environmental factors that influence biological mechanisms that, in turn, affect intelligence scores. One group of these are the prenatal factors. These are factors that affect a child before birth. The two that have received the most attention are smoking and alcohol intake of mothers during pregnancy. Both have an adverse effect on the intelligence of children. Both smoking and drinking alcohol during pregnancy greatly increase the risk of a low-weight baby, and low-weight babies on average show reduced intelligence. One study of over 3000 18- to 19-year-old males showed that those that had mothers who smoked more than 20 cigarettes a day had lower average IQ levels than those that had mothers who did not smoke (Mortenson, Michaelson, Saunders and Reinisch, 2005). If a mother drinks large amounts of alcohol during pregnancy it can cause foetal alcohol syndrome, which includes mental retardation and physical symptoms. In smaller doses alcohol intake by the mother is associated with reduced IQ levels (Neisser, 1997).

Another biological factor is nutrition. Many studies have shown the importance of good nutrition to physical health and growth. This affects the brain and the rest of the nervous system and subsequently intelligence. Good diets can improve intelligence while malnutrition is associated with lower intelligence levels. Oddy et al. (2004) studied over 2000 children from birth to eight years old. They found that those who had been breastfed for more than six months had higher verbal intelligence scores than those that had been breastfed for less than six months. Benton and Roberts (1998) found that children who were given a vitamin-mineral supplement to their diet showed increases in their IQ scores. Children who were given a placebo for the same period did not show the same gains. Although most researchers agree that there are negative effects of malnutrition on intelligence, such effects are not easy to establish. This is largely because it is difficult to separate the effects of malnutrition with the poor socioeconomic conditions it is associated with (Neisser et al., 1996).

Some environmental toxins have negative effects on intelligence. One of these toxins is lead and one of the main reasons for removing lead from petrol was to reduce children's exposure to lead in car fumes (particularly in inner cities). In a 13-year longitudinal study of children growing up near a lead smelting plant, Baghurst et al. (1992) and Tong et al. (1996) found that lead levels were significantly associated with lower IQ scores. This association was significant even when other factors such as socioeconomic status, maternal intelligence and so on were controlled.

Social variables

Another vital group of factors in the development of intelligence are the social factors. These vary widely in nature but the two most researched are the family environment and schooling. The effects of different family environments are very difficult to study. Neisser et al. (1996) point out that children need a certain minimum level of care and that failure to provide that level (through neglect or abuse) leads to many negative effects including intellectual problems. However, beyond the minimum level, the role of the family is unclear. Some researchers such as Scarr (1993) suggest that the family environment does not have much of a role in IQ scores. On the other hand, Gottfried (1984), who used a meta-analysis to assess importance of a number of environmental factors, suggests that factors such as parental involvement and daily stimulation were good predictors of IQ levels. There are other aspects of family that can affect intelligence. For example, Belmont and Marolla (1973) suggest that family size and birth order both have an effect on IQ. They found that larger family size tended to be linked to a lower average IQ score in the children. They also found that IQ decreased with birth order. First-born children had an average IQ that was higher than the second, second born had higher than third born and so on. The findings for family size have not replicated in later studies. However, the findings about birth order have been replicated. The birth order effect may be due to more adult attention to children born earlier in the family. Firstborn children do not share attention with siblings. Children born earlier in the family are also exposed to more adult language and more adult ideas. Sameroff, Seifer, Baldwin and Baldwin (1993) conducted a longitudinal study of 215 children to try to indentify the family risk factors that may be related to low IQ. They identified ten, which include such factors as: mother has a history of mental illness, few positive interactions between mother and child, mother did not go to high school. They calculated that each factor reduced the child's IQ score by 4 points.

As with other social factors it is difficult to establish a cause and effect between schooling and intelligence scores. Evidence suggests that schooling may be both a dependent and an independent variable in relation to intelligence (Neisser et al., 1996). Thus those with a high IQ tend to go to school for longer and going to school increases a range of abilities including IQ scores. In a meta-analysis of the area, Ceci (1991) found a variety of evidence for the positive effects of schooling on IQ. Children of a similar age who go through school a year apart (because of an age criteria for entry) show differences in IQ. Those that have been in school longer have a higher IQ. Children's intelligence test scores drop over the long summer holidays and children with intermittent attendance score lower than those who attend school regularly.

Environmental enrichment

Environmental enrichment is a particular type of social factor in which there has been a deliberate attempt to increase levels of intelligence by providing an enriched social environment. These have been offered as intervention programmes to help disadvantaged children. One of the best-known programmes of environmental enrichment is Operation

Head Start which began in 1965. The focus of the programme was on preschool education and health of children from low-income families in the USA. The evaluation of the Head Start programmes is mixed. Many studies show a marked increase in IQ of children on the programme (for example Lazar and Darlington, 1982) but that this increase was no longer evident when the children were at school.

The Carolina Abecedarian project was a controlled experiment to investigate the effects of early enrichment on disadvantaged children. The children were randomly assigned to either a control group who received no assistance or an 'experimental' group who received high-quality childcare. This group were given an educational programme for five days a week until they were about to start school at aged 5. The children were assessed at ages 3, 4, 5, 6.5, 8, 12, 15 and 21. The mean IQ of children on the programme was consistently higher than those in the control group from ages 3 to 21 (Campbell et al., 2001).

Thinking scientifically → **The 'Mozart effect': science, and a scientific legend**

In 1993, Rauscher, Shaw and Ky published a report in the prestigious journal *Nature* that claimed that listening to Mozart's 'Sonata for Two Pianos in D Major' for ten minutes temporarily increased the spatial intelligence scores of college students by 8–9 IQ points. This apparent significant, temporary increase in intelligence became known as the 'Mozart effect'. Rauscher and Shaw (1998) put forward the hypothesis that listening to complex music improves spatial performance by enhancing neural transmission in the cortex. A further study seemed to find the Mozart effect in rats (Rauscher, Robinson and Jens, 1998). In this study, four groups of rats were exposed to either Mozart (complex music), minimalist music, white noise or no noise both *in utero* and for a short period after birth. The rats that were exposed to Mozart later completed mazes faster with fewer errors than rats in other groups.

Although there was some replication of the results by the original researchers and a few others, many other researchers did not find evidence of an effect of Mozart's music on spatial performance. For example, Steele, Bass and Crook (1999) failed to replicate the original findings and found no Mozart effect. In a meta-analysis of 17 studies, Chabris (1999) found that the original finding of an 8–9 points increase in spatial IQ was an exception; other studies did show some rise in IQ but it was only about 2 points which was not a significant increase.

Steele (2000) suggested that any effect of listening to music was caused by the experimental procedure and was an effect of mood changes or psychological arousal rather that an effect of the music per se. This suggestion seemed to be confirmed by Thompson, Schellenberg and Husain (2001) who measured enjoyment, arousal and mood along with spatial test performance. They claim their findings show that the Mozart effect is an artefact of arousal and mood. This of course does not answer the question of why rats show an apparent Mozart effect. The effect in rats is even more confusing since rats are born deaf and even when their hearing develops, they do not hear most of the notes in the Mozart sonata because they respond to different sound frequencies (Steele, 2003).

The claim to have found an effect followed by scrutiny and counter-claims of others shows the progress of science. However, the widespread impact of the Mozart effect in education and even politics reveals an interesting social phenomenon. Bangerter and Heath (2004) suggest that the Mozart effect became a 'scientific legend'. They define a scientific legend as a 'widespread belief that propagates in society, originally arising from scientific study, but that has been transformed to deviate in essential ways from the understanding of the scientists' (p. 608). The Mozart effect was originally based on a few findings that listening to Mozart had a temporary effect on one aspect of intelligence. This was transformed into a popular belief that listening to complex music had long lasting effects on general intelligence and improved the intellectual development of children. Bangerter and Heath report that the Mozart effect became 'omnipresent in US culture' (p. 609). It became widely reported in the media, it generated many dedicated websites offering advice and products to parents and spawned an industry to apparently help parents increase their children's intelligence. The scientific legend extended into politics and in 1998 the state of Georgia, USA passed a bill to distribute free classical music to new mothers. The state of Florida required all state-funded daycare centres to play some classical music every day (Bangerter and Heath, 2004). The fame of the Mozart effect was not limited to the USA but spread throughout the world.

This huge impact stemmed from a claim, now seemingly disproved by evidence, that listening to Mozart has a temporary effect on one aspect of intelligence. It reveals some of the problems of disseminating research findings in psychology. It is very easy to turn scientific reports into a media story that taps into people's concerns, problems and hopes.

The Flynn effect

Tests of intelligence do not remain fixed. Over time, tests need to be re-normalized (to keep the average at 100) and new tests are developed. As new tests are developed they are standardized and calibrated against old tests. In a survey of tests over time, Flynn (1987) found a sustained effect on intelligence scores. He found a relatively rapid increase in intelligence each decade (on average about 3 points per decade). This sustained increase is known as the **Flynn effect**. For example, when the WAIS test was updated in 1978 a group of participants who had averaged 111.3 on the old test (which was standardized in 1953) scored only 103.8. This implies the average adult IQ showed a rise of 7.5 in 25 years. The effect is not confined to one intelligence test but is found across all the tests Flynn examined. Flynn (1984) initially indentified the IQ rise in the USA but soon found it elsewhere and by 1994 had indentified the effect in 20 countries. In the Netherlands, all male conscripts into the army take a version of the Raven's Progressive Matrices test. The same test was used over a number of years allowing a direct comparison to be made over a thirty-year period. In 1952 the average score on the test was 100 but by 1982 the average was 121.1, an average gain of 7 points per decade.

Neisser (1997) puts these gains into context. Since IQ scores are based on normal distribution only about 5 per cent of the population fall more than two standard deviations from the mean. Thus only 2.5 per cent score above 130 ('very superior') and 2.5 per cent score below 70 ('intellectually deficient'). If we were to compare US Americans taking the Stamford-Binet test in 1932 and 1997 there are vast differences. A group of adults from 1997 taking the test standardized in 1932 would score on average 120 and a quarter of them would be classed as very superior. Conversely, if a group of adults from 1932 were to take the test standardized in 1997 they would score on average 80, and a quarter would appear deficient. Neisser concludes 'taking the tests at face value, we face one of two possible conclusions: Either America is now a nation of shining intellects, or it was then a nation of dolts' (p. 443).

Although intelligence test scores are rising across a range of countries and a range of tests, the rise is not uniform. Flynn (1994) found that the increase was greater on non-verbal tests (such as WICS, WAIS and Raven's) than verbal tests (such as school SAT tests). In other words, the increase was greater on tests measuring abstract problem solving or some form of *g* tests than tests of verbal knowledge.

The cause of the gains is a mystery. Flynn (1987) and others point out that such a rapid rise cannot be explained by genetic changes and therefore represents a particular type of environmental effect. The first question to be addressed is whether increases in IQ scores represent an actual increase in intelligence. Flynn (1994) suggests not. He points out that if the increases in scores represented real gains in intelligence we should be in the midst of a cultural renaissance, but this is not happening. Similarly, Neisser (1997) suggests if the gains in general intelligence were real we would be living in an age of remarkable genius, but the evidence implies otherwise. If the increase in test scores does not represent a real increase in intelligence this still leaves the question 'what causes intelligence test scores to increase?' Flynn (1994) concludes that the tests do not actually measure intelligence but only some abstract problem-solving ability with little practical significance. In contrast, Neisser (1997) does not dismiss the tests but suggests a number of other possible reasons for the increase: test-taking sophistication, length of schooling, parental styles, nutrition and the visual/technical environment.

There has been a steady increase in the number of intelligence tests (or similar tests) that people take. During the first half of the last century many people may have taken either one (on joining the army) or none. Children in school systems now take many such tests, sometimes one a year. Neisser suggests one possible reason for the Flynn effect is test-taking sophistication; we are better at tests because we are used to taking tests. However, if this were the case the increase should be seen most in the type of verbal tests used in schools but is not; the increase is seen in the non-verbal tests. A second reason could be linked to schooling. In countries where the Flynn effect exists there has been an increase in the number of years people study at school and college. Neisser points out that in studies of children who did not go to school the IQ scores dropped, and other studies show increased time at school is linked to higher IQ scores. However, as with the test-taking sophistication argument, increased schooling should be associated more with increases in verbal tests but the increases are in non-verbal.

Neisser notes that the Flynn effect corresponds to changes in child-rearing practices. Parental styles have changed and Neisser observes 'Parents everywhere are now interested in their children's intellectual development and are probably doing more to encourage it than they did in the past' (1997). However, he points to mixed success of early intervention and suggests that the effect of early childhood stimulation is unlikely to be a major factor in the IQ score rises.

During the past century changes in diet and improved nutrition were responsible for improvements in health. During this time in western societies there has been a steady increase in physical factors such as height. Neisser questions whether nutrition might also be responsible for increases in intelligence scores. However, he points out this would imply that the rise in scores represents a genuine increase in intelligence and that we are all much more intelligent than our grandparents' generation. He also notes that there is little evidence of a direct link between diet and intelligence.

Another change in countries where the IQ scores are rising is the increase in exposure to many types of visual media and to technology. Each generation has had a richer visual and technological environment than the last. The increase in visual displays is not merely one of exposure since we use the information rather than merely view it (in picture puzzles, video games and so on). Neisser (1997) points out that each succeeding generation seems better at these skills. These types of skills form part of tests such as Raven's Progressive Matrices. This may account for the increase on non-verbal tests but not verbal tests of intelligence. Neisser believes we may be seeing an increase in visual analysis abilities but not in general intelligence.

Summary

There are many potential environmental influences on intelligence scores. One of the biological factors is the prenatal environment where smoking cigarettes and drinking alcohol are associated with lowered average IQ scores. Nutrition may also play a role in intelligence scores, with good or enriched diets being linked to increases in IQ scores. The effect of the family environment on intelligence is difficult to study as it is hard to separate this from other variables but there does seem to be evidence of a birth order effect. There is a variety of evidence to suggest that schooling increases intelligence test scores and also evidence that enriched environments in preschool years affect IQ throughout childhood. The Flynn effect is the rapid rise in IQ scores found throughout the last century in a number of countries. It seems to be a particular type of environmental effect and, although the exact cause of it is unclear, it is unlikely to represent real gains in general intelligence of the population. One possibility is that the Flynn effect is caused by a richer visual and technological environment, which improves the ability to visually analyse material.

Culture and intelligence

What is regarded as intelligence and intelligent behaviour varies across cultures. The discussion so far has concentrated on notions of intelligence from a western industrial or post-industrial society point of view. This view of intelligence is not shared throughout the world. In a study in California, Okagaki and Sternberg (1993) asked parents about child rearing and children's intelligence. Some parents were native-born Anglo-Americans and others were immigrants from countries such as Mexico, Cambodia and Vietnam. Only the Anglo-Americans focused on cognitive skills; all the others highlighted social skills and motivation as being more important.

Sternberg (2004) points out that it is not just the concept that varies across cultures. He suggests what *is* intelligent in one culture is different to another. He notes 'Intelligence cannot be fully or even meaningfully understood outside its cultural context' (p. 325). For example, the skills I learned to be able to write this book are useful in my culture but would not enable me to adapt to life in the Amazonian rainforest. If there, I am not sure I would be able to find my way beyond a few metres let alone feed or clothe myself. There I would not show much useful intelligent behaviour. Conversely the behaviour of the Yanomami people in the rainforest is intelligent but would not be adapted for a culture that demanded academic skills. Studies of children in different cultural settings have shown how the culture produces demands for different skills (for example Sternberg and Grigorenko, 2004). Serpell (1979) asked Zambian and English children to reproduce wire models, clay models and patterns on paper. The Zambian children (who used wire) did best with the wire models but the English children (who were more familiar with paper and pens) did best with the paper patterns.

However, it is not only that different cultures require different intelligent behaviour; they may lead to different ways of thinking. For example, when asked to sort objects in our culture we tend to do so hierarchically. So a number of animals might be sorted into birds, mammals, fish and so on. However, the Kpelle from West Africa tend to sort objects functionally rather than hierarchically (Cole, Gay, Glick and Sharpe, 1971). They grouped objects that are used together such as knife and fish. When asked to group objects like a fool would do, they grouped them hierarchically! Sternberg uses the example of Puluwat sailors in the Pacific Ocean to illustrate the role of culture in intelligence. The Puluwat sail long distances with no navigational aids and rely on observations of current, cloud and stars. Imagine what their test of intelligence would be like: would anybody from our culture 'pass'? Miller (1997) argues that cultural contexts do not merely provide different opportunities for intellectual development but affect the form they take. She points out that no measure of intelligence is culture-free as effects of prior knowledge cannot be separated from IQ scores. Furthermore, research from a cultural psychology perspective challenges many of the assumptions that underlie behaviour–genetic research. Similarly, Grigorenko and Kornilova (1997) argue that cultural and political biases influence all discussions of heredity versus environment debates. They suggest conclusions from the debate are influenced by the cultural context of the debate.

Group differences and subculture

One of the consistent findings of intelligence tests is that there are differences in the averages of different groups. There is little dispute about these findings and indeed, the APA task force on intelligence report these as part of the 'knowns' of intelligence research (Neisser et al., 1996). However, there is much dispute about what these findings represent and how they are explained. But before examining this controversial dispute, we need to review the findings outlined in the APA report on intelligence. The findings and figures of these 'knowns' are all based on differences in mean scores (that is, there is a lot of overlap in scores). Thus they do not imply all X score higher than Y since their normal distribution curves will overlap considerably.

The APA task force on intelligence began by considering sex differences in intelligence. They found no evidence of overall differences in male and female but they did find evidence of differences in some abilities. Males generally score higher on subscales of visual-spatial tasks such as mental rotation and tracking through space. Females generally do better on subscales of verbal abilities and in school tests achieve better in literature and language. The source of these differences is unclear. The difficulty of finding whether differences are largely genetic or environmental is illustrated by quantitative abilities or the ability to deal with numbers. In early years, females typically score higher on subscales of quantitative abilities but this reverses before puberty and from then on males do better.

The APA task force on intelligence then went on to consider ethnic groups in the USA. This is the most controversial area of intelligence research and is the reason for the heated debate about genetic and environment factors. The APA prefer to use the term groups since the various populations in America are not homogeneous and are largely socially defined (Asian Americans for example could originate from China, Japan, Philippines, India and so on). Studies of African Americans typically report 15 points lower than the Anglo-American population (Jensen, 1980). It is possible that this difference is decreasing as in several studies since 1980 the differential was in single figures. The one standard deviation difference seen in 1978 reduced to 0.65 standard deviations by 1990 because of gains in the African American population. The mean of Hispanic Americans falls between that of the Anglo-American and African American population. One complication with the Hispanic population is language as, for some populations, English is the second not first language. Hispanic children tend to do better on performance than on verbal subscales. The IQ scores of Asian Americans are something of an enigma. Most studies suggest that the average score is slightly less than the Anglo-American population. However, on all scales of achievement Asian Americans score higher than the Anglo-American population.

The controversy surrounding these figures centres on two questions:

1 Do the differences in scores represent actual differences in intelligence between groups?
2 Are the differences in scores caused by genetic factors?

In a book called *The Bell Curve: Intelligence and Class Structure in American Life*, Herrnstein and Murray (1994) answered yes to both questions. They put forward six premises about intelligence:

1 There is a general factor of intelligence
2 The general factor of intelligence is measured best by IQ tests
3 IQ scores reflect what people mean when they refer to intelligence
4 IQ scores are stable over an individual's life
5 If IQ tests are administered correctly there is no bias against any socioeconomic, ethnic or racial groups
6 The cognitive abilities represented by intelligence are largely heritable

These premises lead to a number of conclusions about IQ in the USA. They suggest that at the top end of the distribution of scores there is a cognitive elite emerging. However, at the other end, they suggest that low IQ is the cause of many social and economic problems. This is in contrast to the majority of researchers who tend to suggest that poor socio-economic circumstances are the cause of low IQ scores. Herrnstein and Murray then went on to argue that a large part of the IQ differences between various groups was due to genetic factors. They used this as an argument to stop affirmative action programmes such as Head Start, since in their view it is a waste of money.

Herrnstein and Murray have been widely criticized. Many of the conclusions they reach are based on the six premises (which were presented more as conclusions). However, each of these premises has been challenged. For example, there is no consensus among researchers of intelligence that a general factor exists let alone that it can be best measured by IQ tests. IQ tests are, at best, a sample of a person's intelligence. The APA intelligence report claims there is no direct evidence for the genetic hypothesis of ethnic differences in intelligence. Indeed any evidence that exists tends to suggest no differences. The task force point to the variety of socioeconomic factors that differ between the various ethnic groups in the USA as one likely contributor to IQ score differences. They also suggest that some ethnic groups live, or have lived, in caste-like conditions. In countries where caste systems exist, those in lower castes tend to do worse on IQ tests than those in higher castes. This is not a genetic effect but one of expectation. Lower caste people expect to do worse at everything and this becomes a self-fulfilling prophecy. The APA report suggests this was also the case for some ethnic groups.

Eysenck (2004) makes two important points about the ethnic group and intelligence debate. Firstly, it is impossible to carry out direct research that can inform the debate. It is impossible to quantify the effects of deprivation on the black population in the USA and impossible to compare genetic endowment for intelligence of white and black people. Secondly, evidence for genetic factors in intelligence variation *within* a population does not support the idea that genetic factors play a part in differences *between* populations. He illustrates this point by considering the height of 20 year olds in a country. If we were to measure everyone in that population now we would find a mean height and some variation from the mean. We might estimate that the variation is mostly due to heritability. If we were then to look at records for 20 year olds in the same country 100 years ago we would find the mean height was much less. Despite the high heritability figure this does not mean the genetics of the population has changed. It is the environment that has changed and we simply cannot compare the genetic component of one population (today) with another (100 years ago). The APA task force on intelligence also conclude: 'The fact is, however, that the high heritability of a trait within a given group has no necessary implications for the source of a difference between groups.'

Summary

Culture affects intelligence in many ways. Different cultures have different conceptions of what is meant by intelligence. Any intelligent behaviour depends upon the cultural context it is shown in. Intelligent behaviour in one culture may not be intelligent in another. The cultural context also affects the types of skills the individuals in the culture develop. Different cultures can also lead to different ways of thinking. Any discussion of the heredity versus environment debate must also consider the cultural context.

Many studies show that there are differences in IQ levels of various groups. Although there are no overall differences between males and females, there are differences in the visual-spatial and verbal subscales. In some countries, such as the USA, there are differences between various cultural groups. For example, the mean scores of both the African American and the Hispanic American groups tend to be lower than the Anglo-American group. The reasons for these differences in IQ are not known. However the claim by Herrnstein and Murray, that the scores represent actual differences in intelligence and that these differences have a genetic basis, has caused much controversy. Critics point out that IQ scores only represent a sample of a person's intelligence and that differences between mean scores have many socioeconomic causes. They also stress that the estimates of a genetic component from within a population cannot be applied between populations.

Interaction of genetics and environment

The evidence about causes of variability in intelligence has been presented as either genetic or environmental. However, as noted at the beginning of the chapter, neither of these factors acts in isolation, they interact. Sternberg and Grigorenko (1997) suggest there are three facts about variability in intelligence that seem to be almost universally accepted. Firstly, both heredity and environment contribute to intelligence. Secondly, heredity and environment interact and do so in a variety of ways. Thirdly, both extremely poor and extremely rich environments affect a person's intelligence regardless of their genetic potential. However, there the agreement ends and beyond these three facts there is a great divergence of opinion. In a book called *Intelligence, Heredity, and Environment*, Sternberg and Grigorenko (1997) gathered together views of leading researchers that represent this diversity of views.

One view is that evidence suggests that differences in intelligence test scores are largely caused by genetic factors. For example, Scarr (1997) suggests that socialization theories of intelligence are not supported by data and that the data is better explained by behaviour genetics. Similarly, Bouchard (1997) argues that the evidence of similarities in IQ scores between MZ twins reared apart cannot be explained by any other factor than genetics. He suggests that criticisms to the conclusions from behaviour genetics fall into two classes: pseudo-analyses and pseudo-arguments.

In contrast, Gordon and Lemons (1997) believe many people have overestimated the contribution of genetics to IQ variation. They suggest the debate between genetics and environment is unproductive and that an interactionist approach sheds far more light on the subject than either extreme alone. Bidell and Fischer (1997) also point out that it is a mistake to try to separate the source of variation in intelligence into two categories of heredity and environment. These factors cannot be seen as separate but as related systems that are integrated. They claim that the basic technique of behaviour genetics of portioning intelligence into heritability and environment is fundamentally flawed. They point out we actively interact with our environments to make sense of the world. Therefore any explanation of human skills and differences in skills needs to be interpreted at a variety of levels including biological, cognitive-behavioural and sociocultural. Hunt (1997, p. 549) concludes:

> we inherit blueprints for constructing proteins; all else follows from interactions! What we need to do is to understand the causal pathway at both the molecular genetics and psychological-social ends of the continuum between genes and culture.

The APA task force on intelligence (Neisser et al. 1996) highlighted a number of 'knowns and unknowns'. The unknowns include:

1 The nature of the genetic contribution to intelligence variation, particularly why the impact of genetics seems to increase with age
2 The nature of the environmental contribution to intelligence variation. This includes knowing what the environmental factors are or how they work
3 The cause of the rise in intelligence scores (the Flynn effect)
4 How are the aspects of intelligence that are not measured by traditional tests (which include creativity, practical sense, social sensitivity and so on) related to traditional conceptions of intelligence?

These unknowns represent the consensus opinion of many of the leading researchers in the field. This seems to suggest that the debate about the cause of intelligence variation is set to continue for some time.

Summary

There is a consensus that both genetics and environment play a part in intelligence variation and that these two factors interact. However, beyond that there is disagreement. Some believe the evidence points to a largely genetic explanation of intelligence differences. Others believe it is a mistake to try to separate the source of variation in intelligence into two categories of heredity and environment. They suggest we should adopt an interactive approach that includes a variety of factors including socio-cultural. The APA task force on intelligence suggest there are a number of unknowns about intelligence variation. These include the contribution of genetics and environment.

Further reading

Neisser, U., Boodoo, G., Bouchard, T.J., Boykin, A.W., Brody, N., Ceci, S.J., Halpern, D.F., Loehlin, J.C., Perloff, R., Sternberg, R.J. and Urbina, S. (1996) 'Intelligence: knowns and unknowns'. *American Psychologist*, 51, 77–101.

This is the report of the APA task force on intelligence. It represents the consensus opinions of leading researchers in the USA. It summarizes research into:

- Conceptions of intelligence (covered in Chapter 6)
- Intelligence tests and test performance
- Genes and intelligence
- Environmental effects on intelligence
- Group differences

Summaries of the work can be found online using 'APA task force on intelligence' in a search.

Sternberg, R.J. and Grigorenko, E.L. (eds) (1997) *Intelligence, Heredity, and Environment.* Cambridge: Cambridge University Press.

Glossary

Anthropomorphism describing and explaining animal behaviour in human terms.

Behaviour shaping also known as successive approximations, this is the teaching of a new behaviour in gradual stages until a target behaviour is achieved.

Blocking in classical conditioning, if a new stimulus is combined with a previously conditioned stimulus then little conditioning occurs to the new stimulus.

Concurrent validity a type of validity that assesses a measure by comparing it to another, accepted measure of the same construct.

Conditioned response (CR) the response to the conditioned stimulus alone.

Conditioned stimulus (CS) a stimulus that triggers the same response as the unconditioned stimulus after being paired with it.

Crystallized intelligence (Gc) intelligence represented by acquired knowledge and skills.

Displacement the ability to talk about things that are not present.

Emotional intelligence the intelligence needed to understand and manage one's own and others' emotions.

Encephalization quotient (EQ) a quotient that reflects brain size relative to body size. It is found by comparing the ratio of brain to body size of a species with the ratio for similar species.

Environment of evolutionary adaptation (EEA) the environment in which a particular behaviour evolved.

External reliability refers to the consistency of a measure across different measurements. It is often assessed using the test-retest method.

Extinction the gradual decline and disappearance of the CR to the CS when it is no longer paired with the unconditioned stimulus (UCS).

Face validity the type of validity that occurs when a measure appears to be measuring the appropriate construct.

Fluid intelligence (Gf) the ability to solve abstract problems.

Flynn effect the continued increase in intelligence test scores.

General intelligence or '*g*' a general underlying intelligence that determines abilities in all spheres.

Hominin a group of species that includes modern humans and their direct, extinct ancestors.

Insight learning learning that uses cognitive processes such as reason to solve a problem.

Intelligence quotient the score from standardized tests of intelligence which has an average value of 100.

Internal reliability refers to the internal consistency of a test and whether all the items are measuring the same thing.

Latent learning learning in the absence of reinforcement which is demonstrated when reinforcement is given.

Lloyd Morgan's Canon if behaviour can be explained by both a simple and a complex process, then the simpler explanation should be accepted.

Machiavellian intelligence this type of intelligence is related to living in groups. It refers to the ability to manipulate other animals, to form advantageous alliances with other animals and sometimes to use deception to achieve your own ends.

Negative reinforcement this occurs when a behaviour is followed by the removal of an aversive stimulus (which increases the likelihood that the behaviour will be repeated).

Neocortex the outer layer of the cerebral hemispheres which is involved in higher cognitive functions.

Positive reinforcement this occurs when a behaviour is followed by a favourable stimulus (which increases the likelihood that the behaviour will be repeated).

Predictive validity a type of validity that assesses whether a measure predicts some future behaviour.

Prevarication the ability to use language to lie and talk about impossibilities.

Primary reinforcer also known as unconditioned reinforcer, this is a stimulus that reinforces behaviour naturally (for example food, water, and so on).

Productivity the ability to use language to produce and understand a vast number of messages.

Punishment this occurs when a behaviour is followed by an aversive stimulus (which decreases the likelihood that the behaviour will be repeated).

Reflex involuntary response to a stimulus.

Reinforcement this occurs when something that follows a behaviour makes the behaviour more likely to be repeated.

Reinforcer anything that, following behaviour, makes that behaviour more likely to happen again.

Reliability the consistency of a measure.

Savants savant syndrome refers to a condition where people with developmental or intellectual disorders show gifts in one particular field.

Secondary reinforcer also known as conditioned reinforcer, this is a stimulus that becomes reinforcing because of an association with a primary reinforcer (for example money).

Semanticity the ability of language to convey meaning.

Spontaneous recovery the reappearance of the CR after extinction without further pairing of the UCS and CS.

Stimulus discrimination the process of eliciting the CR to a narrower range of stimuli.

Stimulus enhancement the increase in the likelihood that an animal will approach an object after seeing another interact with it.

Stimulus generalization the tendency of the CR to be produced by stimuli that are similar to the CS.

Theory of mind the ability to attribute mental states to oneself and others.

Traditional transmission the learning of a language from one generation to the next.

Unconditioned response (UCR) a response to a stimulus that is automatic and involuntary (reflex).

Unconditioned stimulus (UCS) a stimulus that triggers an automatic (unconditioned) response.

Upper Paleolithic Revolution a period in the development of humans that is characterized by the emergence of culture (cave art, figurines and so on).

Validity is concerned with whether a test actually measures what it is intended to measure.

References

Aiello, L.C. and Dunbar, R.I.M. (1993) Neocortex size, group size and the evolution of language. *Current Anthropology,* 34, 184–93.

Aiello, L.C. and Wheeler, P. (1995) The expensive-tissue hypothesis: the brain and the digestive system in human and primate evolution. *Current Anthropology*, 36, 199–221.

Aiello, L.C. (1996) Terrestiality, bipedalism and the origins of language. *Proceedings of the British Academy,* 88, 269–89.

Alexander, R.D. (1989) Evolution of the human psyche. In P. Mellars and C. Stringer (eds), *The Human Revolution: Behavioral and Biological Perspectives on the Origins of Modern Humans* (pp. 455–513) Princeton: Princeton University Press.

Anderson, M. (1992) *Intelligence and Development: A Cognitive Theory*. Oxford: Blackwell.

Anderson, M. (ed.) (1999) *The Development of Intelligence*. Hove: Psychology Press.

Ash, J. and Gallup Jr., G.G. (2007) Paleoclimatic variation and brain expansion during human evolution. *Human Nature,* 18, 109–24.

Baghurst, P.A., McMichael, A.J., Wigg, N.R., Vimpani, G.V., Robertson, E.F., Roberts, R.J. and Tong, S.L. (1992) Environmental exposure to lead and children's intelligence at the age of seven years: the Port Pirie cohort study. *New England Journal of Medicine,* 327, 79–86.

Bailey, D.H. and Geary, D.C. (2009) Hominid brain evolution: Testing climatic, ecological and social competition models. *Human Nature,* 20, 67–79.

Bangerter, A. and Heath, C. (2004) The Mozart effect: Tracking the evolution of a scientific legend. *British Journal of Social Psychology,* 43, 605–23.

Bar-On, R. (2004) The Bar-On Emotional Quotient Inventory (EQ-i): Rationale, description and summary of psychometric properties. In G. Geher (ed.), *Measuring Emotional Intelligence: Common Ground and Controversy* (pp. 111–42) Hauppauge, NY: Nova Science Publishers.

Bar-On, R. (2006) The Bar-On model of emotional-social intelligence (ESI) *Psicothema*, 18, suppl., 13–25.

Bar-On, R., Brown, J.M., Kirkcaldy, B.D. and Thome, E.P. (2000) Emotional expression and implications for occupational stress: An application of the Emotional Quotient Inventory (EQ-i). *Journal of Personality and Individual Differences*, 28, 1107–18.

Bar-On, R., Tranel, D., Denburg, N. L. and Bechara, A. (2003) Exploring the neurological substrate of emotional and social intelligence. *Brain*, 126, 1790–800.

Barrett, L., Dunbar, R. and Lycett, J. (2002) *Human Evolutionary Psychology*. Basingstoke: Palgrave Macmillan.

Barrett, L., Henzi, P. and Rendall, D. (2007) Social brains, simple minds: does social complexity really require cognitive complexity? In N. Emery, N. Clayton and C. Frith (eds), *Social Intelligence: From Brain to Culture*. Oxford: Oxford University Press.

Bartholomew, D.J. (2004) *Measuring intelligence: Facts and Fallacies*. Cambridge: Cambridge University Press.

Belmont, L. and Marolla, F.A. (1973) Birth order, family size and intelligence. *Science,* 182, 1096–101.

Benson, E. (2003) Intelligent intelligence testing. *APA Monitor on Psychology,* 34, 48.

Benton, D. and Roberts, G. (1988) Effect of vitamin and mineral supplementation on intelligence of a sample of schoolchildren. *Lancet,* i, 140–4.

Bidell, T.R. and Fischer, K.W. (1997) Between nature and nurture: The role of human agency in the epigenesist of intelligence. In R.J. Sternberg and E.L. Grigorenko (eds), *Intelligence, Heredity and Environment.* Cambridge: Cambridge University Press.

Bitterman, M.E. (1975) The comparative analysis of learning: Are the laws of learning the same in all animals? *Science,* 188, 699–709.

Boesch, C. (1991) Teaching in wild chimpanzees. *Animal Behaviour,* 41, 530–2.

Bolles, R.C. (1972) Reinforcement, expectancy and learning. *Psychological Review*, 77, 32–48.

Bonner (1969) Hormones in social amoebae and mammals. *Scientific American*, 220, 78–87.

Bouchard, T.J. Jr. (1997) IQ similarity in twins reared apart: Findings and responses to criticsa. In R.J. Sternberg and E.L. Grigorenko (eds), *Intelligence, Heredity and Environment*. Cambridge: Cambridge University Press.

Bouchard, T.J. Jr. and McGue, M. (1981) Familial studies of intelligence: A review. *Science*, 212, 1055–9.

Bouton, M.E. (2007) *Learning and Behaviour: A Contemporary Synthesis*. Sunderland, MA: Sinauer Associates.

Brace, C.L. (1996) Review of *The Bell Curve*. *Current Anthropology*, 37, 5157–61.

Brown, R. (1973) *A First Language: The Early Stages*. Cambridge, MA: Harvard University Press.

Buller, D.J. (2005) Evolutionary psychology: the emperor's new paradigm. *Trends in Cognitive Science*, 9, 277–83.

Buller, D.J. (2009) Evolution of the mind: 4 fallacies of psychology. *Scientific American*, January, 60–7.

Buss, D.M. (1995) Evolutionary psychology: A new paradigm for psychological science. *Psychological Inquiry*, 6, 1–30.

Byrne, R.W. and Bates, L.A. (2007) Sociality, Evolution and Cognition. *Current Biology*, 17, 714–23.

Byrne, R.W. and Whiten, A. (eds) (1988a) *Machiavellian Intelligence: Social Expertise and the Evolution of Intellect in Monkeys, Apes and Human*. Oxford: Oxford University Press.

Byrne, R.W. and Whiten, A. (1988b) Tactical deception of familiar individuals in baboons. In R.W. Byrne and A. Whiten (eds), *Machiavellian Intelligence: Social Expertise and the Evolution of Intellect in Monkeys, Apes and Human*. Oxford: Oxford University Press.

Call, J. (2001) Chimpanzee social cognition. *Trends in Cognitive Sciences*, 9, 388–93.

Call, J. (2006) Descartes' two errors: Reason and reflection in the great apes. In S. Hurley and M. Nudds (eds), *Rational Animals*. Oxford: Oxford University Press.

Campbell, F.A., Pungello, E.P., Miller-Johnson, S., Burchinal, M. and Ramey, C. T. (2001) The development of cognitive and academic abilities: Growth curves from an early childhood educational experiment. *Developmental Psychology*, 37, 231–42.

Carroll, J.B. (1993) *Human Cognitive Abilities*. Cambridge: University of Cambridge Press.

Carroll, J.B. (1997) The three-stratum theory of cognitive abilities. In D.P. Flanagan, J.L. Genshaft and P.L. Harrison (eds), *Contemporary Intellectual Assessment: Theories, Tests and Issues* (pp. 122–30) New York: The Guilford Press.

Cattell, R.B. (1971) *Abilities: Their Structure, Growth and Action*. Boston: Houghton-Mifflin.

Ceci, S.J. (1991) How much does schooling influence general intelligence and its cognitive components? A reassessment of the evidence. *Developmental Psychology*, 27, 703–22.

Chabris, C.F. (1999) Prelude or requiem for the 'Mozart effect'? *Nature*, 400, 826–7.

Cheney, D.L. and Seyfarth, R.M. (1999) Recognition of other individuals' social relationships by female baboons. *Animal Behaviour*, 58, 67–75.

Chiappe, D. and MacDonald, K. (2005) The evolution of domain-general mechanisms in intelligence and learning. *The Journal of General Psychology*, 132, 5–40.

Chomsky, N. (1972) *Language and Mind*. New York: Harcourt Brace Jovanovich.

Cole, M., Gay, J., Glick, J. and Sharp, D.W. (1971) *The Cultural Context of Learning and Thinking*. New York: Basic Books.

Connor, R.C. (2007) Dolphin social intelligence: complex alliance relationships in bottlenose dolphins and a consideration of selective environments for extreme brain size evolution in mammals. In N. Emery, N. Clayton and C. Frith (eds), *Social Intelligence: From Brain to Culture*. Oxford: Oxford University Press.

Cosmides, L. and Tooby, J. (2002) Unraveling the enigma of human intelligence: Evolutionary psychology and the multimodular mind. In R.J. Sternberg and N.J. Kaufman (eds) *The Evolution of Intelligence* (pp. 145–98) Mahwah, NJ: Lawrence Erlbaum Associates.

Darwin, C. (1981) *The Descent of Man and Selection in Relation to Sex*. London: John Murray.

Davies, M., Stankov, L. and Roberts, R.D. (1998) Emotional intelligence: In search of an elusive construct. *Journal of Personality and Social Psychology*, 75, 989–1015.

De Waal, F.B.M. (1986) The brutal elimination of a rival among captive male chimpanzees. *Ethology and Sociobiology,* 7, 237–51.

Deary, I. (1992) Multiple minds. *Science,* 259, 28.

Dunbar, R.I.M. (1993) The co-evolution of neocortical size, group size and language in humans. *Behavioral and Brain Sciences,* 16, 681–735.

Dunbar, R.I.M. (1997) Groups, gossip and the evolution of language. In A. Schmitt, K. Atzwanger, K. Grammer and K. Schafer (eds), *New Aspects of Human Ecology* (pp. 77–90) New York: Plenum Press.

Dunbar, R.I.M. (1998) The social brain hypothesis. *Evolutionary Anthropology,* 6, 178–90.

Eichenbaum, H. (2008) *Learning and Memory*. New York, NY: W.W. Norton & Company.

Evans, D.M. and Martin, N.G. (2000) The validity of twin studies. *GeneScreen,* 1, 77–9.

Eysenck, M.W. (2004) *Psychology: An International Perspective*. Hove: Psychology Press.

Fabrigar, L.R., Wegener, D.T., MacCallum, R.C. and Strahan, E.J. (1999) Evaluating the use of exploratory factor analysis in psychological research. *Psychological Methods,* 4, 272–99.

Fish, J.L. and Lockwood, C.A. (2003) Dietary constraints on encephalization in primates. *American Journal of Physical Anthropology,* 120, 171–81.

Fisher, J.A. (1996) The Myth of Anthropomorphism. In M. Bekoff and D. Jamieson (eds) *Readings in Animal Cognition*. Cambridge, MA: The MIT Press.

Flavell, J.H. (1979) Metacognition and cognitive monitoring: A new area of cognitive-developmental inquiry. *American Psychologist,* 34, 906–11.

Flinn, M.V., Geary, D.C. and Ward, C.V. (2005) Ecological dominance, social competition and coalitionary arms races: Why humans evolved extraordinary intelligence. *Evolution and Human Behavior,* 26, 10–46.

Flynn, J.R. (1984) The mean IQ of Americans: massive gains. *Psychological Bulletin,* 95, 29–51.

Flynn, J.R. (1987) Massive IQ gains in 14 nations: what IQ tests really measure. *Psychological Bulletin,* 101, 171–91.

Flynn, J.R. (1994) IQ gains over time. In R.J. Sternberg (ed.) *Encyclopedia of Human Intelligence* (pp. 617–23) New York: Macmillan – now Palgrave Macmillan.

Follesdal, H. and Hagtvet, K.A. (2009) Emotional Intelligence: The MSCEIT from the Perspective of Generalizability Theory. *Intelligence*, 37, 94–105.

Fouts, R.S., Hirsch, A.D. and Fouts, D.H. (1982) Cultural transmission of a human language in a chimpanzee mother–infant relationship. In H.E. Fitzgerald, J.A. Mullins and P. Gage (eds) *Child Nurturance: III, Studies of Development in Nonhuman Primates.* New York: Plenum.

Galef, B.G. Jr. (1980) Diving for food: Analysis of a possible case of social learning in wild rats (*Rattus norvegicus*). *Journal of Comparative and Physiological Psychology,* 94, 416–25.

Galef, B.G. Jr. (1988) Communication of information concerning diets in social central-place foraging species: *Rattus norvegicus*. In T.R. Zentall, & B.G. Galef Jr (eds), *Social learning psychological and biological perspectives* (pp. 119–40) Hillsdale, NY: Lawrence Erlbaum Associates.

Galef, B.G. Jr., Lee, W.Y. and Whiskin, E.E. (2005) Lack of interference in long-term memory for socially learned food preferences in rats (*Rattus norvegicus*). *Journal of Comparative Psychology,* 119, 131–5.

Garcia, J. and Koelling, R.A. (1966) Relation of cue to consequence in aviodance learning. *Psychonomic Science,* 4, 123–4.

Garcia, J., Rusiniak, K.W. and Brett, L.P. (1977) Conditioned food-illness in wild animals: *Caveant canonici*. In H. Davis and H.M.B. Hurwitz (eds), *Operant-Pavlovian Interactions* (pp. 273–316) Hillsdale, NY: Lawrence Erlbaum Associates.

Gardner, H. (1983) *Frames of Mind: The Theory of Multiple Intelligences.* New York: Basic Books.

Gardner, H. (1993) *Creating Minds: An Anatomy of Creativity as Seen Through the Lives of Freud, Einstein, Picasso, Stravinsky, Elliot, Graham and Gandhi*. New York: Basic Books.

Gardner, H. (1998) Are there additional intelligences? The case for naturalist, spiritual and existential intelligences. In J. Kane (ed.), *Education, Information and Transformation* (pp. 111–32) Englewood Cliffs, NJ: Prentice Hall.

Gardner, H. (1999) *Intelligence Reframed. Multiple Intelligences for the 21st Century*. New York: Basic Books.

Gardner, H. (2002) Three distinct meanings of intelligence. In R.J. Sternberg, J. Lautrey and T.I. Lubard (eds) *Models of Intelligence:*

International Perspectives. Washington, DC: American Psychological Society.

Gardner, H. (2006) *Multiple Intelligences: New Horizons*. New York: Basic Books.

Gardner, H., Kornhaber, M.L. and Wake, W.K. (1996) *Intelligence: Multiple Perspectives*. Fort Worth, TX: Harcourt Brace College.

Gardner, R.A. and Gardner, B.T. (1969) Teaching sign language to a chimpanzee. *Science,* 165, 664–72.

Geary, D.C. (2005) *The Origins of Mind: Evolution of Brain, Cognition and General Intelligence.* Washington, DC: American Psychological Association.

Goleman, D. (1995) *Emotional Intelligence: Why it Can Matter More Than IQ*. New York: Bantam Books.

Gordon, E.W. and Lemons, M.P. (1997) An interactionist perspective on the genesis of intelligence. In R.J. Sternberg and E.L. Grigorenko (eds), *Intelligence, Heredity and Environment*. Cambridge: Cambridge University Press.

Gottfried, A.W. (ed.) (1984) *Home Environment and Early Cognitive Development: Longitudinal Research*. New York: Academic Press.

Greenfield, P.M. and Savage-Rumbaugh, E.S. (1990) Grammatical combination in *Pan paniscus:* Process of learning and invention in the evolution and development of language. In S.T. Parker and K.R. Gibson (eds), *'Language' and Intelligence in Monkeys and Apes: Comparative Developmental Perspectives.* New York: Cambridge University Press.

Griffin, A.S. (2004) Social learning about predators: A review and prospectus. *Learning & Behavior,* 32, 131–40.

Grigorenko, E.L. and Kornilova, T.V. (1997) The resolution of the nature-nurture controversy by Russian Psychology: Culturally biased or culturally specific? In R.J. Sternberg and E.L. Grigorenko (eds), *Intelligence, Heredity and Environment*. Cambridge: Cambridge University Press.

Guthrie, E.R. (1935) *The Psychology of Learning*. New York: Harper.

Harcourt, A.H. (1992) Coalitions and alliances: Are primates more complex than non-primates? In A.H. Harcourt and F.B.M. de Waal (eds), *Coalitions and Alliances in Humans and Other Animals*. Oxford: Oxford University Press.

Harcourt, A.H. and de Waal, F.B.M. (eds) (1992) *Coalitions and Alliances in Humans and Other Animals*. Oxford: Oxford University Press.

Harley, T. (2001) *The Psychology of Language: From Data to Theory* (2nd edn). Hove: Psychology Press.

Hayes, K.H. and Hayes, C. (1951) Intellectual development of a house-raised chimpanzee. *Proceedings of the American Philosophical Society,* 95, 105–9.

Herman, L.M. (2002) Vocal, social and self imitation by bottlenosed dolphins. In K. Dautenhan and C.L. Nehanir (eds), *Imitation in Animals and Artefacts* (pp. 63–107) Boston, MA: Bradford Books.

Herman, L.M. (2006) Intelligence and rational behaviour in the bottlenosed dolphin. In S. Hurley and M. Nudds (eds), *Rational Animals*. Oxford: Oxford University Press.

Herman, L.M. and Morrel-Samuels, P. (1996) Knowledge acquisition and asymmetry between language comprehension and production: Dolphins and apes as general models for animals. In M. Bekoff and D. Jamieson (eds) *Readings in Animal Cognition*. Cambridge, MA: The MIT Press.

Herman, L.M., Pack, A.A. and Morrel-Samuels, P. (1993) Representational and conceptual skills of dolphins. In L.M. Roitblat, L.M. Herman and P.E. Nachtigall (eds), *Language and Communication: Comparative Perspectives.* Hillsdale, NJ: Lawrence Erlbaum Associates.

Herman, L.M., Richards, D.G. and Wolz, J.P. (1984) Comprehension of sentences by bottlenosed dolphins. *Cognition,* 16, 129–219.

Herrnstein, R. and Murray, C. (1994) *The Bell Curve: Intelligence and Class Structure in American Life.* New York: Free Press.

Heyes, C.M. (1998) Theory of mind in nonhuman primates. *Behavioral and Brain Sciences,* 21, 101–48.

Hinde, R.A. and Fisher, J. (1951) Further observations on the opening of milk bottles by birds. *British Birds,* 44, 392–6.

Hockett, P.C. (1960) The origins of speech. *Scientific American*, 203, 89–96.

Holekamp, K.E., Sakai, S.T. and Lundrigan, B.L. (2007) Social intelligence in the spotted hyena (*Crocuta crocuta*). In N. Emery, N. Clayton and C. Frith (eds), *Social Intelligence: From Brain to Culture*. Oxford: Oxford University Press.

Howe, M.J.A. (1997) *IQ in Question: The Truth about Intelligence*. London: Sage.

Humphrey, N.K. (1976) The social function of intellect. In P.P.G Bateson and R.A. Hinde (eds), *Growing Points in Ethology*. Cambridge: Cambridge University Press.

Hunt, E. (1997) Nature vs. nurture: The feeling of *vujà dé*. In R.J. Sternberg and E.L. Grigorenko (eds), *Intelligence, Heredity and Environment*. Cambridge: Cambridge University Press.

Jaeggi, A.V., Dunkel, L.P., Van Noordwijk, M.M., Wich, S.A., Sura, A.A. and Van Schaik, C.P. (2009) Social learning of diet and foraging skills by wild immature Bornean orangutans: implications for culture. *American Journal of Primatology*, 71, 1–10.

Jensen, A.R. (1980) *Bias in Mental Testing*. New York: Free Press.

Jensen, A.R. (1998) *The g Factor: The Science of Mental Ability*. Westport, CT: Praeger.

Jensen, A.R. (2009) Book review of 'Howard Gardner under fire: The rebel psychologist faces his critics, Jeffrey A Schaler (ed.), (2006), Chicago and La Salle, Illinois: Open Court'. *Intelligence*, 36, 96–7.

Kamin, L.J. (1969) Selective association and conditioning. In N.J. Mackintosh and W.K Honig (eds), *Fundamental Issues in Associative Learning*. Halifax: Dalhouse University Press.

Kamin, L.J. and Goldberger, A.S. (2002) Twin studies in behavioural research: A sceptical view. *Theoretical Population Biology*, 61, 83–95.

Kawai, M. (1965) Newly-acquired pre-cultural behavior of the natural troop of Japanese Monkeys on Koshima Islet. *Primates*, 6, 1–30.

Kellogg, W.N. and Kellogg, L.A. (1933) *The Ape and the Child*. New York: McGraw Hill.

King, B.J. (1986) Extractive foraging and the evolution of primate intelligence. *Human Evolution*, 1, 361–72.

Kluemper, D.H. (2008) Trait emotional intelligence: The impact of core-self evaluations and social desirability. *Personality and Individual Differences*, 44, 1402–12.

Kohler, W. (1925) *The Mentality of Apes*. New York: Harcourt.

Kuhn, T.S. (1996) *The Structure of Scientific Revolutions* (3rd edn). Chicago: Chicago University Press.

Lazar, I. and Darlington, R. (1982) Lasting effects of early education: A report from the Consortium for Longitudinal Studies. *Monographs of the Society for Research in Child Development*, 49.

Lewin, R. (1991) Look who's talking now. *New Scientist*, 27th April, 48–52.

Lissman, H.W. (1963) Electric location by fishes. *Scientific American*, 207, 50–9.

Loehlin, J.C., Horn, J.M. and Willerman, L. (1997) Heredity, environment and IQ in the Texas Adoption Project. In R.J. Sternberg and E.L. Grigorenko (eds), *Intelligence, Heredity and Environment.* Cambridge: Cambridge University Press.

Loehlin, J.C. and Nichols, R.C. (1976) *Heredity, Environment and Personality*. Austin, TX: Texas University Press.

Lund, N. (2003) *Language and Thought*. Hove: Routledge.

Mackintosh, N.J. (1998) *IQ and Human Intelligence*. Oxford: Oxford University Press.

Macphail, E.M. (1985) Vertebrate intelligence: The null hypothesis. In L. Weiskrantz (ed.), *Animal Intelligence*. Oxford: Clarendon.

McQuoid, L.M. and Galef, B.G. Jr. (1992) Social influences on feeding site selection by Burmese fowl (*Gallas gallus*). *Journal of Comparative Psychology,* 106, 136–41.

Marshall-Pescini, S. and Whiten, A. (2008) Social learning of nut-cracking behavior in East African sanctuary-living chimpanzees (*Pan troglodytes schweinfurthii*). *Journal of Comparative Psychology,* 122, 186–94.

Martin, N., Boomsma, D. and Machin, E. (1997) A twin-pronged attack on complex traits. *Nature Genetics,* 17, 387–92.

Matlin, M.W. (2009) *Cognition* (7th edn). Hoboken, NJ: Wiley.

Mayer, J.D. and Salovey, P. (1997) What is emotional intelligence? In P. Salovey and D. Sluyter (eds) *Emotional Development and Emotional Intelligence: Implications for Educators* (pp. 3–31) New York: Basic Books.

Mayer, J.D., Caruso, D. and Salovey, P. (1999). Emotional intelligence meets traditional standards for an intelligence. *Intelligence,* 27, 267–98.

Mayer, J.D., Salovey, P. and Caruso, D.R. (2002) *Mayer-Salovey-Caruso Emotional Intelligence Test (MSCEIT)*. Toronto: Multi-Health Systems.

Mayer, J.D., Salovey, P. and Caruso, D.R. (2004) Emotional intelligence: Theory, findings and implications. *Psychological Inquiry,* 15, 197–215.

Miller, G. (2000) *The Mating Mind: How Sexual Choice Selection Shaped the Evolution of the Human Mind*. New York: Doubleday.

Miller, J.G. (1997) The cultural-psychology perspective on intelligence. In R.J. Sternberg and E.L. Grigorenko (eds), *Intelligence, Heredity and Environment*. Cambridge: Cambridge University Press.

Mineka, S. and Cook, M. (1988) Social learning and the acquisition of snake fear in monkeys. In T.R. Zentall and B.G. Galef Jr. (eds) *Social Learning Psychological and Biological Perspectives* (pp. 51–74) Hillsdale, NY: Lawrence Erlbaum Associates.

Morgan, C.L. (1894) *An Introduction to Comparative Psychology.* London: Scott.

Mortenson, E.L., Michaelson, K.F., Saunders, S.A. and Reinisch, J.M. (2005) A dose-response relationship between maternal smoking in late pregnancy and intelligence in male offspring. *Paediatric and Perinatal Epidemiology,* 19, 4.

Nagell, K., Olguin, R.S. and Tomasello, M. (1993) Processes of social learning in the tool use of chimpanzees (*Pan troglodytes*) and human children (*Homo sapiens*). *Journal of Comparative Psychology,* 107, 174–86.

Naglieri, J.A. and Das, J.P. (1997) *Cognitive Assessment System: Interpretive Handbook*. Itasca, IL: Riverside.

Nakajima, S., Arimitsu, K. and Lattal, K.M. (2002) Estimation of animal intelligence by university students in Japan and the United States. *Anthrozoos,* 15, 194–205.

Neisser, U. (1997) Rising scores on intelligence tests. *American Scientist,* 85, 440–7.

Neisser, U., Boodoo, G., Bouchard, T.J., Boykin, A.W., Brody, N., Ceci, S.J., Halpern, D.F., Loehlin, J.C., Perloff, R., Sternberg, R.J. and Urbina, S. (1996) Intelligence: knowns and unknowns. *American Psychologist*, 51, 77–101.

Oddy, W.H., Sherriff, J.L., de Klerk, N.H., Kendall, G.E., Sly, P.D., Beilin L.J. Blake, K.B., Landau, L.I. and Stanley, F.J. (2004) The relation of breastfeeding and body mass index to asthma and atopy in children: A prospective cohort study to age 6 years. *American Journal of Public Health,* 94, 1531–7.

Okagaki, L. and Sternberg, R.J. (1993) Parental beliefs and children's school performance. *Child Development*, 64, 36–56.

Olson, D.J., Kamil, A.C., Balda, R.P. and Nims, P.J. (1995) Performance of four seed-caching corvid species in operant tests of nonspatial and spatial memory. *Journal of Comparative Psychology,* 109, 173–81.

Palmer, B.R., Gignac, G., Manocha, R. and Stough, C. (2005) A psychometric evaluation of the Mayer-Salovey-Caruso Emotional Intelligence Test Version 2.0. *Intelligence,* 33, 285–305.

Patterson, F.G. (1978) Linguistic capabilities of a lowland gorilla. In F.C.C. Peng (ed.), *Sign Language and Language Acquisition in Man and Ape: New Dimensions in Comparative Pedolinguistics.* Boulder, CO: Westview Press.

Patterson, F.G. (1980) Innovative uses of language by a gorilla: A case study. In Nelson, K. (ed.), *Children's Language,* Vol. 2. New York: Gardner Press.

Patterson, F.G. and Linden, E. (1981) *The Education of Koko.* New York: Holt, Rinehart & Winston.

Patterson, F.G and Matevia, M.L. (2001) Twenty-seven years of Project Koko and Michael. In B.M.F. Galdikas, N.E. Briggs, L.K. Sheeran, G.L. Shapiro and J. Goodall. *All Apes Great and Small: African Apes* (pp. 165–76) Springer.

Pavlov, I.P. (1927) *Conditioned Reflexes.* Oxford: Oxford University Press.

Pearce, J.M. (2008) *Animal Learning and Cognition: An Introduction* (3rd edn). Hove: Psychology Press.

Penn, D.C. and Povinelli, D.J. (2007) On the lack of evidence that non-human animals possess anything remotely resembling a 'theory of mind'. In N. Emery, N. Clayton and C. Frith (eds), *Social Intelligence: From Brain to Culture.* Oxford: Oxford University Press.

Pfungst, O. (1965) *Clever Hans: The Horse of Mr Van Osten.* New York: Holt.

Plomin, R. (1990) *Nature and Nurture: An Introduction to Human Behavioral Genetics.* Pacific Grove, CA: Brooks/Cole Publishing.

Plotnik, J.M., de Waal, F.B.M. and Reiss, D. (2006) Self-recognition in an Asian elephant. *Proceedings of the National Academy of Science of the USA,* 103, 17053–7.

Popper, K.R. (1959) *The Logic of Scientific Discovery.* London: Hutchinson.

Povinelli, D.J. and Eddy, T.J. (1996) What young chimpanzees know about seeing. *Monographs of the Society for Research in Child Development,* 61, 1–190.

Povinelli, D.J., Gallup, G.G. Jr., Eddy, T.J., Bierschwale, D.T., Engstrom, M.C., Perilloux, H.K. and Toxopeus, I.B. (1997) Chimpanzees recognise themselves in mirrors. *Animal Behaviour,* 53, 1083–8.

Povinelli, D.J., Nelson, K.E. and Boysen, S.T. (1990) Inferences about guessing and knowing by chimpanzees (*Pan troglodytes*). *Journal of Comparative Psychology,* 108, 74–80.

Povinelli, D.J., Parks, K.A. and Novak, M.A. (1991) Do rhesus monkeys (*Macaca mulatta*) attribute knowledge and ignorance to others? *Journal of Comparative Psychology,* 105, 318–25.

Povinelli, D.J., Rulf, A.B., Landau, K.R. and Bierschwale, D.T. (2003) Self-recognition in chimpanzees (*Pan troglodytes*): Distribution, ontogeny and patterns of emergence. *Journal of Comparative Psychology,* 107, 347–72.

Povinelli, D.J. and Vonk, J. (2003) Chimpanzee minds: Suspiciously human? *Trends in Cognitive Sciences,* 7, 157–60.

Premack, D. (1971) Language in a chimpanzee? *Science,* 172, 808–22.

Premack, D. (1976) *Intelligence in Ape and Man.* Hillsdale, NJ: Lawrence Erlbaum Associates.

Premack, D. and Woodruff, G. (1978) Does the chimpanzee have a theory of mind? *Behavioral and Brain Sciences,* 4, 515–26.

Premack, D. (2004) Is language key to human intelligence? *Science,* 303, 318–20.

Prior, H., Schwarz, A. and Güntürkün, O. (2008) Mirror-induced behavior in the magpie (*Pica pica*): Evidence of self-recognition. *PLoS Biology,* 6(8): e202. doi:10.1371/journal.pbio.0060202.

Rauscher, F.H., Robinson, K.D. and Jens, J. (1998) Improved maze learning through early music exposure in rats. *Neurological Research,* 20, 427–32.

Rauscher, F.H. and Shaw, G.L. (1998) Key components of the Mozart effect. *Perceptual and Motor Skills,* 86, 835–41.

Rauscher, F.H., Shaw, G.L. and Ky, K.N. (1993) Music and spatial task performance. *Nature,* 365, 611.

Record, R.G., McKeown, T. and Edwards, J.H. (1970) An investigation of the difference in the measured intelligence between twins and single births. *Annals of Human Genetics,* 34, 11–20.

Reiss, D. and Marino, L. (2001) Mirror self-recognition in the bottlenose dolphin: A case of cognitive convergence. *Proceedings of the National Academy of Sciences,* 98, 5937–42.

Rescorla, R.A. and Wagner, A.R. (1972) A theory of Pavlovian conditioning: Variations in the effectiveness of reinforcement and nonreinforcement. In A.H. Black and W.F. Prokasy (eds), *Classical Conditioning II: Current Research and Theory*. New York: Appleton-Century-Crofts.

Ridley, M. (1999) *Genome: The Autobiography of a Species in 23 Chapters.* London: Fourth Estate.

Rivas, E. (2005) Recent use of signs by chimpanzees (*Pan troglodytes*) in interactions with humans. *Journal of Comparative Psychology,* 119, 404–17.

Roberts, W.A. (1998) *Principles of Animal Cognition*. Boston, MA: McGraw-Hill.

Roth, G. and Dicke, U. (2005) Evolution of the brain and intelligence. *Trends in Cognitive Sciences,* 9, 250–7.

Rumbaugh, D.M. (1977) *Language Learning by a Chimpanzee: The LANA project.* New York: Academic Press.

Rumbaugh, D.M. and Savage-Rumbaugh, E.S. (1994) Language in comparative perspective. In N.J. Mackintosh (ed.) *Animal Learning and Cognition.* London: Academic Press.

Russon, A.E. and Galdikas, B.M.F. (1993) Imitation in free-ranging rehabilitant orangutans (*Pongo pygmaeus*). *Journal of Comparative Psychology,* 107, 147–61.

Salovey, P. and Mayer, J.D. (1990) Emotional intelligence. *Imagination, Cognition and Personality,* 9, 185–211.

Salovey, P. and Pizarro, D.A. (2002) The value of emotional intelligence. In R.J. Sternberg, J. Lautrey and T.I. Lubard (eds) *Models of Intelligence: International Perspectives.* Washington, DC: American Psychological Society.

Sameroff, A.J., Seifer, R., Baldwin, A. and Baldwin, C. (1993) Stability of intelligence from preschool to adolescence: The influence of social and family risk factors. *Child Development,* 64, 80–97.

Savage-Rumbaugh, E.S. (1986) *Ape Language: From Conditioned Response to Symbol.* New York: Columbia University Press.

Savage-Rumbaugh, E.S. and Brakke, K.E. (1996) Animal language: methodological and interpretive issues. In M. Bekoff and D. Jamieson (eds) *Readings in Animal Cognition.* Cambridge, MA: The MIT Press.

Savage-Rumbaugh, E.S., Murphy, J., Sevcik, R.A., Brakke, K.E., Williams, S.L. and Rumbaugh, D.M. (1993) Language comprehension in ape and child. *Monographs of the Society for Research in Child Development,* 58, 1–256.

Savage-Rumbaugh, E.S., Rumbaugh, D.M. and Fields, W.M. (2006) Language as a window on rationality. In S. Hurley and M. Nudds (eds), *Rational Animals.* Oxford: Oxford University Press.

Scarr, S. (1985) An author's frame of mind: Review of *Frames of Mind* by Howard Gardner. *New Ideas in Psychology,* 3, 95–100.

Scarr, S. (1989) Protecting general intelligence: Constructs and consequences for interventions. In R.I. Linn (ed.) *Intelligence: Measurement, Theory and Public Policy.* Chicago: University of Illinois Press.

Scarr, S. (1993) Biological and cultural diversity: The legacy of Darwin for development. *Child Development,* 64, 1333–53.

Scarr, S. (1997) Behavior-Genetic and Socialization theories of intelligence: Truce and reconciliation. In R.J. Sternberg and E.L. Grigorenko (eds), *Intelligence, Heredity and Environment*. Cambridge: Cambridge University Press.

Schaie, K.W. (1996) *Intellectual Development in Adulthood: The Seattle Longitudinal Study*. Cambridge: Cambridge University Press.

Seligman, M.E.P. (1970) On the generality of the laws of learning. *Psychological Review*, 77, 406–18.

Serpell, R. (1979) How specific are perceptual skills? A cross-cultural study of pattern reproduction. *British Journal of Psychology*, 70, 365–80.

Seyfarth, R.M. and Cheney, D.L. (1986) Vocal development in vervet monkeys. *Animal Behaviour*, 34, 1640–58.

Seyfarth, R.M., Cheney, D.L. and Marler, P. (1980) Monkey responses to three different alarm calls: Evidence of predator classification and semantic communication. *Science*, 210, 801–3.

Shanker, S.G., Savage-Rumbaugh, E.S. and Taylor, T.J. (1999) Kanzi: a new beginning. *Animal Learning and Behaviour*, 27, 24–6.

Sherry, D.F. and Galef, B.G. Jr. (1984) Social learning without imitation: more about milk bottle opening by birds. *Animal Behaviour*, 40, 987–9.

Shettleworth, S.J. (1998) *Cognition, Evolution and Behaviour*. New York: Oxford University Press.

Shettleworth, S.J. and Sutton, J.E. (2006) Do animals know what they know? In S. Hurley and M. Nudds (eds), *Rational Animals*. Oxford: Oxford University Press.

Shields, J. (1962) *Monozygotic Twins*. Oxford: Oxford University Press.

Skinner, B.F. (1938) *The Behaviour of Organisms*. New York: Appleton-Century-Crofts.

Skinner, B.F. (1948) 'Superstition' in the pigeon. *Journal of Experimental Psychology*, 38, 168–72.

Skinner, B.F. (1977) Why I am not a cognitive psychologist. *Behaviorism*, 5, 1–10.

Smith, J.D. (2009) The study of animal metacognition. *Trends in Cognitive Sciences*, 13, 389–96.

Spearman, C. (1923) *The Nature of Intelligence and the Principles of Cognition*. London: Macmillan.

Spink, A. and Cole, C. (2007) Information behavior: A socio-cognitive ability. *Evolutionary Psychology*, 5, 257–74.

Steele, K.M. (2000) Arousal and mood factors in the 'Mozart effect'. *Perception and Motor Skills*, 91, 188–90.

Steele, K.M. (2003) Do rats show a Mozart effect? *Music Perception,* 21, 251–65.

Steele, K.M., Bass, K.E. and Crook, M.D. (1999) The mystery of the Mozart effect: Failure to replicate. *Psychological Science,* 10, 366–9.

Sternberg, R. J. (1977): *Intelligence, information processing,and analogical reasoning: The componential analysis of human abilities*. Hillsdale, NJ: Erlbaum.

Sternberg, R.J. (1983) Components of human intelligence. *Cognition,* 15, 1–48.

Sternberg, R.J. (1985) *Beyond IQ: A Triarchic Theory of Human Intelligence*. New York: Cambridge University Press.

Sternberg, R.J. (1991) Death, taxes and bad intelligence tests. *Intelligence,* 15, 257–70.

Sternberg, R.J. (1997) Educating intelligence: Infusing the Triarchic Theory into school education. In R.J. Sternberg and E.L. Grigorenko (eds), *Intelligence, Heredity and Environment*. Cambridge: Cambridge University Press.

Sternberg, R.J. (2002) Construct validity of the theory of successful intelligence. In R.J. Sternberg, J. Lautrey and T.I. Lubard, (eds) *Models of Intelligence: International Perspectives*. Washington, DC: American Psychological Society.

Sternberg, R.J. (2004) Culture and Intelligence. *American Psychologist,* 59, 325–38.

Sternberg, R.J., Conway, B.E., Ketron, J.L. and Bernstein, M. (1981) People's conception of intelligence. *Journal of Personality and Social Psychology,* 41, 37–55.

Sternberg, R.J. and Detterman, D.K. (eds) (1986) *What is Intelligence? Contemporary Viewpoints on its Nature and Definition*. Norwood, NJ: Ablex.

Sternberg, R.J. and Grigorenko, E.L. (eds) (1997) *Intelligence, Heredity and Environment*. Cambridge: Cambridge University Press.

Sternberg, R.J. and Grigorenko, E.L. (2004) Intelligence and culture: how culture shapes what intelligence means and the implications for a science of well-being. Philosophical Transactions of the Royal Society of London, 1427–34.

Sternberg, R.J. and Kaufman, J.C. (1998) Human abilities. *Annual Review of Psychology,* 49, 479–502.

Sternberg, R.J. and Kaufman, J.C. (eds) (2002) *The Evolution of Intelligence*. Mahwah, NJ: Lawrence Erlbaum Associates.

Sternberg, R.J., Lautrey, J. and Lubard, T.I. (eds) (2002) *Models of Intelligence: International Perspectives*. Washington, DC: American Psychological Society.

Sternberg, R.J. and The Rainbow Project Collaborators (2006) The Rainbow Project: Enhancing the SAT through assessments of analytical, practical and creative skills. *Intelligence,* 34, 321–50.

Strum, S.C., Forster, D. and Hutchins, E. (1997) Why Machiavellian intelligence may not be Machiavellian. In A. Whiten and R.W. Byrne (eds) *Machiavellian Intelligence II: Extensions and Evaluations*. Cambridge: Cambridge University Press.

Terrace, H.S. (1979) *Nim*. New York: Knopf.

Terrace, H.S., Petitto, L.A., Sanders, R.J. and Bever, T.G. (1979) Can an ape create a sentence? *Science,* 206, 891–900.

Thompson, W.F., Schellenberg, E.G. and Husain, G. (2001) Arousal, mood and the Mozart effect. *Psychological Science,* 12, 248–51.

Thorndike, E.L. (1911) *Animal Intelligence: Experimental Studies*. New York: Macmillan.

Thurstone, L.L. (1938) *Primary Mental Abilities*. Chicago, IL: University of Chicago Press.

Toda, K. and Watanabe, S. (2008) Discrimination of moving video images of self by pigeons (*Columba livia*). *Animal Cognition,* 11, 699–705.

Tolman, E.C. and Honzik, C.H. (1930) 'Insight' in rats. *University of California Publications in Psychology,* 4, 215–32.

Tomasello, M., Call, J. and Hare, B. (2003) Chimpanzees understand psychological states – the question is which ones and to what extent? *Trends in Cognitive Sciences,* 7, 152–6.

Tomasello, M. and Call, J. (2006) Do chimpanzees know what others see – or only what they are looking at? In S. Hurley and M. Nudds (eds), *Rational Animals?* Oxford: Oxford University Press.

Tong, S.L., Baghurst, P., McMichael, A., Sawyer, M. and Mudge, J. (1996) Life time exposure to environmental lead and children's intelligence at 11–13 years: The Port Pirie Cohort Study. *British Medical Journal,* 312, 1569–75.

Tooby, J. and Cosmides, L. (2005) Conceptual foundations of evolutionary psychology. In D.M. Buss (ed.), *The Handbook of Evolutionary Psychology*. Hoboken NJ: Wiley.

Tyack, P. (1983) Differential response of humpback whales *Megaptera novaengliae* to playback of song or social sounds. *Behavioural Ecology,* 13(1): 49–55.

Vernon, P.E. (1971) *The Structure of Human Abilities*. London: Methuen.

Visser, B.A., Ashton, M.C. and Vernon, P.A. (2006a) Beyond *g*: Putting multiple intelligences theory to the test. *Intelligence,* 34, 487–502.

Visser, B.A., Ashton, M.C. and Vernon, P.A. (2006b) *g* and the measurement of multiple intelligences: A response to Gardner. *Intelligence,* 34, 507–10.

von Frisch, K. (1950) *Bees, their Vision, Chemical Senses and Language.* Oxford: Oxford University Press.

von Frisch, K. (1974) Decoding the language of the bee. *Science,* 185, 663–8.

Wahlsten, D. and Gottlieb, G. (1997) The invalid separation of the effects of nature and nurture: Lessons from animal experimentation. In R.J. Sternberg and E.L. Grigorenko (eds), *Intelligence, Heredity and Environment*. Cambridge: Cambridge University Press.

Wallman, J. (1992) *Aping Language.* Cambridge: Cambridge University Press.

Warren, J.M. (1973) Learning in vertebrates. In D.A. Dewsbury and D.A. Rethlingshafer (eds), *Comparative Psychology: A Modern Survey* (pp. 471–509) New York: McGraw-Hill.

Watson, J.B. and Rayner, R. (1920) Conditioned emotional reactions. *Journal of Experimental Psychology,* 76, 82–8.

Whiten, A. and Byrne, R.W. (eds) (1997) *Machiavellian Intelligence II: Extensions and Evaluations*. Cambridge: Cambridge University Press.

Whiten, A., Custance, D.M., Gomez, J.C., Teixidor, P. and Bard, K.A. (1996) Imitative learning of artificial fruit processing in children (*Homo sapiens*) and chimpanzees (*Pan troglodytes*). *Journal of Comparative Psychology* 110, 3–14.

Willingham, D.T. (2004) Check the facts: Reframing the mind. *Education Next,* 4, 18–24.

Wolfe, J.B. (1936) Effectiveness of token-rewards for chimpanzees. *Comparative Psychology,* 12(60).

Woodruff, G. and Premack, D. (1979) Intentional communication in the chimpanzee: The development of deception. *Cognition,* 7, 333–62.

Yang, S. and Sternberg, R.J. (1997) Taiwanese Chinese people's conceptions of intelligence. *Intelligence,* 25, 21–36.

Yodlowski, M.L., Kreithen, M.L. and Keeton, W.T. (1977) Detection of atmospheric infrasound by homing pigeons. *Nature,* 265, 725–6.

Index

Entries in **bold** refer to glossary definitions

M

N

O

P

R

Reading guide

This table identifies where in the book you'll find relevant information for those of you studying or teaching A-level. You should also, of course, refer to the Index and the Glossary, but navigating a book for a particular set of items can be awkward and we found this table a useful tool when editing the book and so include it here for your convenience.

	Specification		Page
Topic	AQA(A)	WJEC	
Adoption studies		x	133
Brain size	x		79–81
Classical conditioning	x		12
Ecological demands	x		84
Environmental factors – test performance	x		135
Evolutionary factors – development	x	x	84–93
Family studies		x	130
Gardner – multiple intelligences	x	x	105–9
Genetic factors	x	x	130–5
Influence of culture		x	143
Information processing theory	x		111–20
IQ testing	x	x	98
Learning approach	x		1–2, 5–9, 32–3
Machiavellian intelligence	x		33, 42–4
Measurement of intelligence	x	x	98
Operant conditioning	x		21
Prenatal factors		x	135
Psychometric theory	x	x	98–105
Self-recognition	x		49–52

	Specification		Page
Topic	**AQA(A)**	**WJEC**	
Social complexity	x		88
Social learning	x		36–42
Spearman – two-factor theory		x	100
Thurstone – multifactor theory		x	100
Twin studies		x	131–3